WHERE
THE
LANGUAGE
LIVES

ʔəshəliʔ ti dxʷləšucid
Lushootseed Lives!

To Father Pat,
    Thank you for all of the loving support you gave to Vi during her life and for your continued support of Lushootseed.   With great respect,
                                                    Janet

WHERE
THE
LANGUAGE
LIVES

VI HILBERT AND THE
GIFT OF LUSHOOTSEED

JANET YODER

Janet Yoder

GFB

GIRL FRIDAY BOOKS

GIRL FRIDAY BOOKS

Published by Girl Friday Books™, Seattle
www.girlfridaybooks.com

Produced by Girl Friday Productions

Development & editorial: Devon Fredericksen
Editorial production: Jaye Whitney Debber
Cover design: Danielle Christopher

All photos courtesy of Lushootseed Research, unless otherwise noted:
Brad Burns: 95
Chris Duenas / Puyallup Tribal Language Program: 203
Paul Eubanks: Cover, 43 (portrait of Vi Hilbert), 48, 49 (top), 84, 140, 188
Eugene H. Field / University of Washington Libraries: 106 (bottom)
Ron Hilbert: 37 (bottom)
Sasha La Pointe: 173
Chris Leman / EastlakeInfo.Net: 150 (bottom)
Carolyn Michael: xi, 172, 193, 207
Jay Miller: 72 (bottom), 106 (top)
Robby Rudine: iii (based on photo by Paul Eubanks), 12,
    33 (top), 43, 60, 61, 62, 83 (bottom), 129, 135 (used with
    permission from the artist Susan A. Point), 154
Jay Samson: 120-122
Kenneth Greg Watson: 94, 150 (top), 216
Janet Yoder: 63 (top)

ISBN (paperback): 978-1-954854-26-0
ISBN (e-book): 978-1-954854-51-2

Library of Congress Control Number: 2021925827

First edition

CONTENTS

FOREWORD

This collection of essays beautifully chronicles the thirty-year friendship between the author and my grandmother, which started in a classroom and grew into a lifelong familial connection. Janet Yoder takes us on a visual journey with each of her essays, recounting experiences so vividly that at times it feels as though we are right there experiencing them alongside her.

The stories shared in this collection wrap us in a colorful and vibrant tapestry of topics centered around the rich cultural life of *taqʷšəblu*, Vi Hilbert. *taqʷšəblu* was a distinguished member of the Upper Skagit Indian Tribe in northwest Washington State. She was a great-great-grandmother, a teacher, a scholar, and an internationally renowned storyteller. She was beloved and revered by many, both in Indigenous tribal communities and in broader diverse communities throughout the world. *taqʷšəblu* has been credited for saving her nearly dormant Indigenous language—Lushootseed—though she would give credit to the wonderful elders, scholars, and volunteers who contributed to her life's work in a multitude of ways. It has been said that nearly everyone who can speak Lushootseed today either learned it directly from *taqʷšəblu* or learned it from one of her students.

The essays capture both humorous and subtle teachings about traditional wisdoms and expectations designed to help us navigate our ever-changing world. The cultural lessons and values embedded throughout this collection demonstrate the author's profound and intimate appreciation for *taqʷšəblu*'s culture and her unwavering commitment to her work.

For *taqʷšəblu*, preservation of the language, culture, and ancestral wisdom was foremost in all her endeavors. She carried herself in a way that her elders would have approved of. She strove to embody the traditional teachings she was entrusted to carry and share by example. Even when the old family home she had grown up in at Nooksack was destroyed by a fire decades later, she was compelled to call upon traditional healers to take care of the home in a spiritual manner, as described in the essay "Burning at Nooksack."

While many of Janet's essays illuminate *taqʷšəblu*'s public persona, others more intimately capture *taqʷšəblu*'s vulnerable and human frailties, which were visible neither to her general audiences nor to her adoring students. She was not immune to all the heartaches and disappointments of this world—and she endured her fair share—yet she remained strong and resilient. Her strength and determination were a testament to her parents, who raised her with the tremendous expectation—which she consistently rose to—that she was the best, but no better than anyone else.

Jill La Pointe, *tsisqʷux̌ʷaʔɬ*

ᒍᔿᒢ

To read these essays was a gift. As *taqʷšəblu*'s great-granddaughter, I was touched to feel her presence in these pages. Janet truly knew my great-grandmother, and through the closeness the two of them shared over decades of friendship comes an honest and intimate portrait of a woman who meant so much to so many. I am honored to have known Janet for nearly my entire life. My

great-grandmother embraced her as family, and throughout
the years I've had the pleasure of getting to know Janet at intimate family gatherings as well as Lushootseed Research events.
Whether enjoying salmon baked in my great-grandparents'
backyard or devoting her time to language events, Janet has been
a part of our family and a part of my great-grandmother's life
for as long as I can remember. In a way, reading these pages
brought her back to us. This book feels like a true celebration
of who my great-grandmother was and the wonderful things she
accomplished.

Sasha La Pointe, *taqʷšəblu*

Vi Hilbert and granddaughter Jill La Pointe (photo by Carolyn Michael)

INTRODUCTION

How do you know when you meet the teacher who will change your life? I met Vi Hilbert in the fall of 1978 when I walked into her Lushootseed class at the University of Washington. She was sixty and I was twenty-seven. Though petite and soft-voiced, Vi was a presence. She stood in front of the class and lifted her arms to welcome us as if this room were her home. Vi introduced herself to us: "I am *taqʷšəblu* (TAWKW-shuh-blue)." The room was full of students. Some tribal people, some linguists, some just curious, some completing an academic requirement. I fell into the last category, needing to take two quarters of a non-Indo-European language in order to earn a master of arts in teaching English as a second language. My advisor suggested Arabic or Japanese. I opened the course catalog, saw Lushootseed, and that was that.

I knew Lushootseed would be interesting simply because it was the language of Chief Seattle, for whom my city is named. Surely the language would reveal something of the culture of the First People of this particular place. But who was Vi Hilbert? How was it that she spoke the language when few others did? What would I learn from her?

During that academic year, I learned some of the Lushootseed language and stories, both of which gave a view into the traditions

of the culture. Later I became one of Vi's volunteers. As an out-
sider, I know there is much that I will never know. But to Vi
Hilbert, it was important to introduce her volunteers to aspects
of the culture, inviting us to witness canoe races, bone games,
naming ceremonies, ritual burnings, and winter spirit dancing.
She wanted us to understand her drive to preserve the language
and see how it was intertwined with the traditions. This was a
huge gift to us. It also helped us become better, more respectful
volunteers. Over the next thirty years, I learned what I could
from the language, the stories, the culture, and the spirit. More
important, I learned from Vi Hilbert, from how she lived her life.

Lushootseed stretched my mind and my mouth. I struggled
to pronounce the shushes, clicks, and scratchy sounds from the
back of the throat. Even to say *I am fine* (*ʔəƛubil čəd*) required a
minor explosion on either side of my tongue. I did my homework,
spoke when Vi called on me, learned how to say *King Salmon is
swimming upriver. Elk is on the other side of the river. Bear is
on this side of the road.* I learned numbers, learned to say *father,
mother, sister, brother, aunt, uncle, grandma,* and *grandpa.* I
learned to say *I have three sisters and no brother.* But I kept
thinking that Lushootseed was sadly doomed. It was only spoken
by a few elders and not spoken much by children. What could be
done? The odds against Lushootseed seemed too great. The fact
that I thought this meant I didn't yet really know Vi Hilbert.

I kept coming to Lushootseed class and brought Robby Rudine
(now my husband) with me. Robby excelled at Lushootseed. He
could not get enough of it. He asked Vi the kinds of questions
she loved to be asked: how to say things she had never said in
Lushootseed, what to call a computer, a printer, a postage stamp.
Or how to seek the etymology of a term—for example, does the
word for *traditional healer* come from the root word for *naming*? Without Robby, I fear I might have lost touch with Vi. With
Robby, I volunteered time to help Vi with her work in whatever
way we *pastəd* (non-tribal people) could. Over time, Vi invited

us into her world. Over time, she became a mentor, and over more time, a treasured friend.

So begins my story of spending time with Vi Hilbert. Her lifework was the preservation of her native language—Lushootseed—and the culture it expresses. She taught the language, transcribed old recordings, translated those recordings into English, and published books of this work. She spoke at gatherings and told stories, all in Lushootseed. Vi made it a priority to make her work accessible to the public and especially to tribal people. She inspired those around her to help with the work, to take on the project that each was meant to do. Some have become Lushootseed teachers in their own right. Many tribes now offer Lushootseed classes for both children and adults. You can hear the language spoken at gatherings and see it written in public places throughout Seattle and the greater Puget Sound, our home on the Salish Sea.

Vi's importance to me grew over time spent with her at Paddle to Seattle, at the Tulalip Longhouse for Treaty Day, at the Lummi Reservation for the Stommish canoe races, at naming ceremonies, and at ritual burnings. It came over years of observing how Vi carried herself in Indian Country or when speaking to a room full of psychiatrists, schoolteachers, or scholars, or to those gathered at Seattle's Northwest Folklife Festival. It came from watching her find just the right story to share with a specific gathering, the story they needed to hear. It came from years spent with Vi—digging clams at her beach property, eating salmon cooked by the fire her husband and son tended, driving to a Salish Conference, or just going shopping. Vi loved shopping.

Over time, I recorded numerous conversations with Vi about her life, her Lushootseed work, and her culture. I transcribed those conversations and out of them came this book, one essay at a time. These recordings are part of the Vi Hilbert Collection in the University of Washington Ethnomusicology Archives. Excerpts of these recordings can be heard at the university's website honoring her life and work: "Voices of the First People: Audio and Video Recordings from the Vi Hilbert Collection."

Some essays in this book were published during Vi's lifetime and with her approval. Each time, Vi received the first copy, and she immediately made a hundred copies to give out at her birthday party or next gathering. Late in her life, Vi called me her chronicler. The truth is that many in Vi Hilbert's world have written about her, spoken about her, and been inspired by her. There will be more to come.

Where the Language Lives is not a definitive biography of Vi Hilbert. It is not the only book about or inspired by Vi. Nor will it be the last. Vi's great-granddaughter Sasha La Pointe is a superb writer. Her work takes my breath away. Sometimes it calls on what she carries of Vi, including her traditional name, *taqʷšəblu*. Sasha is one to watch and follow.

Where the Language Lives is my account of what it was like to know Vi from 1978 to 2008, to observe her, listen to her, go places with her, be in some way part of her world. It is my way of bearing witness to all that she shared with me and with others. Writing this book is a way of completing the work Vi gave me and of thanking her for including me so often that she shaped the person I became. I have tried to do this with respect for the culture Vi introduced me to and with honorable intentions.

I have written about Vi because writing is my currency of appreciation. I owe her more than I can say. I offer words on paper, in the same way that I might bring her Skagit corn when it is sweetest, make her a pot of chili, or give her a pair of down booties to warm her feet. I write about Vi to remember her fully, to share her with others. I write about Vi to try to understand what it means to live in Seattle, a city right in the center of Lushootseed language territory. I write about Vi to remind myself how to conduct my life. I feel blessed and sometimes amazed by her friendship and the generosity with which she shared her traditions with those around her and with a larger world. I write about Vi to hold her in my heart.

Vi Hilbert in her Seattle home (photo courtesy Lushootseed Research)

WHERE THE
LANGUAGE LIVES

In my late twenties, I entered the University of Washington to study the process of language learning and earn a master of arts in teaching English as a second language. To understand the challenges my students faced learning a language unrelated to their own, I enrolled in a class called Puget Sound Salish (Lushootseed). Listed under "foreign" languages, Lushootseed was the native language of Chief Seattle and the First People of western Washington between the shores of Puget Sound (part of the Salish Sea) and the Cascade Mountains, from the Skagit River in the north down to Mud Bay in the south. Except for abundant place names, *sockeye* and *geoduck* are the only words I know that have made the journey from Lushootseed into English. I hoped following the trail into Lushootseed might offer a glimpse of the rich world it describes.

That first day, Vi greeted me as I entered her Denny Hall classroom. A petite, smooth-skinned Native American woman in her sixties, Vi wore a red blouse, a long, black skirt, and slim leather boots. She stood facing us, arms at her side, palms outward in what I would learn to recognize as a gesture of welcome. Her soft, clear voice addressed us first in Lushootseed, then in English. "Welcome, dear ones. I am *taqʷšəblu*, Vi Hilbert, of Upper Skagit. I thank you for coming here to study Lushootseed." She presented her language, which had only recently arrived in print. Inside our thick homemade textbooks we found drawings of animals from the time when they were people who could talk to each other, play tricks on each other, and teach each other lessons. That first day, we learned to name each animal and its location in the world. *That is Eagle. Eagle is in the tree. There is Salmon. Salmon is in the river.* Weeks passed before we learned the words for *book, notebook, pen,* and *desk.* The word for *clock* didn't enter the picture for months.

We struggled to wrap our mouths around the explosive clicks and thick, throaty sounds. We practiced speaking a hard *k* or *q* sound followed by a soft blowing wind. We learned to say our names and where we came from. Native students were *ʔaciɬtalbixʷ* (people), further identified by tribal affiliation, like Tulalip, Skokomish, Snohomish, or Muckleshoot; the rest of us learned to say we were *pastəd* (the Lushootseed pronunciation of *Boston,* the origin place of the first Europeans in this region). We told each other we were well, hungry, thirsty, or tired. "I am twenty-seven years old and have three little sisters and a cat." We added words as we went. We took Lushootseed dictation, watching Vi's mouth with the rapt attention of hungry baby hawks. We wrote our homework using the Lushootseed orthography based on the International Phonetic Alphabet, the notation system that gave every sound its place on paper. Every day, Vi stood in front of us, welcoming us formally into her class and thanking us at the end. She always addressed us with the words of respect: *siʔab* for a man or *tsi siʔab* for a woman. Likely we all wondered whether we could possibly deserve the respect her words bestowed.

Gradually Vi Hilbert's Lushootseed class became its own world, complete with our own Coyote trickster, a ladies' man

Mink, a slumbery Bear, an industrious Blue Jay, and a bewildered Deer. For an hour a day, we became an academic version of the world of the animals who were people. Once we played *sləhal*, a bone game, that calls on the bluffing power of one team to prevent opponents from divining which hand holds the unmarked deer bone versus the one marked with two black bands. Our teams encouraged and distracted each other with drumming and singing of rowdy bone game songs.

Even as I delighted in learning a bit of Lushootseed, I lamented what I perceived as the loss of the whole language. Vi shared tape recordings of speakers who were no longer with us, those who claimed Lushootseed as their first language, possibly their only language. Those voices boomed through time, with the confidence of fluency and linguistic complexity. They did not pause to search for a missing word. Vi hesitated at times, as if traveling back for an ancestral vocabulary check. Finding it, she spoke and we noted her words on paper. I recognized the need for linguistic triage to prevent the bleeding out of this language, yet I continued my academic path, completed my degree, and took a teaching job in Portland, where the Oregon Trail ended, where between the 1840s and 1860s, four hundred thousand settlers crossed the continent and forever changed the Northwest Coast.

꜕ℾꜝ

In my thirties, I taught English to students from the Arabias, Asia, and Latin America. In my classes, students entered English and learned to say *I am hungry. Are you sleepy? How old are you? Where are you from?* I helped them approach American culture as well. I brought in my guitar, played folk songs, and planned field trips to a bowling alley, courtroom, county fair, and even the horse races. My effort and theirs combined to yield a more than reasonable success. At some point, I realized I had adopted something of Vi's presence in the classroom—welcoming each student, thanking them at the close of class, granting them the respect Vi had shown us.

The gratification of teaching was enough for a time. Students passed through my classroom each quarter, rounds of them with names like Mohammed, Ahmed, Hiroshi, Chieko, Soon Li, Carlos, and Emilia. I did my best to connect with each student and to teach effectively, but I sometimes wondered about the churn of students. My efforts created more speakers of English, the monster language that devoured smaller languages, ones that described one piece of land where everything began and ended. Those worlds were shrinking as the languages that described them went silent.

I returned to Seattle four years later and married Robby, an artist and builder. We were drawn deeper into Vi's world and she lifted her arms to welcome us. Her face had a few new lines but her posture was strong. She glowed with the status of elder, storyteller, and speaker. Robby took the language class again and I joined the Lushootseed literature class to consider the exploits of Coyote, Raven, Skunk, Octopus Lady, and the Basket Ogress. We learned about how Bear and Ant battled to see whether we would have Bear's one long day of summer and a night as long as winter hibernation or we would have night and then day, night and then day. We went on to the epic story of Star Child and how the world came to be.

Vi brought recordings of speakers giving the story in the old words. She invited a few volunteers to the Longhouse at Tulalip to witness the winter spirit dancing and hear the language spoken by elders around the fires in that great cedar house. She taught us that the ways of the people were still practiced, that not everything had been swallowed by the advance of time or the growing number of *pastəd*. We went on driving trips with Vi to visit the story places. At Mount Si, we saw where the Bird Men pushed off to swing across the valley, leaving their footprints on the side of the mountain. Then we went to *yəyduʔ* (the swing), a rock formed when the cedar bough ladder the sisters Tupaltxw and Yaslibc used to climb down from the Sky World fell into a pile. On the Duwamish River in South Seattle near the Boeing airplane plant, we visited the place where North Wind and South Wind battled for supremacy. At each site, Vi stood to remind us of what happened there, telling us the story again.

In 1987, Vi was about to retire from the university. Linguists rushed to take her class one last time. So did Native and other students alike. A volunteer videotaped each class and no one missed a session. We knew that Vi would not offer it again, that we had to receive the gift as fully as we could.

But receiving the gift was not enough. As the year closed, a group of volunteers met at Vi's house, gathering around her long brown Formica dining table, as if climbing into a family canoe for a journey. "Let's continue the work," we said. Lushootseed Research was four years old. It was time for the *Lushootseed Newsletter.* Then Lushootseed Press, which would publish books of the stories, with place names fully mapped out, and accounts of elders now gone, first in the original Lushootseed, then leaping across the page into English.

Though it was not my nature to step forward, I found myself editing books: *Writings about Vi Hilbert by Her Friends* and then *Lady Louse Lived There.* The linguists among us created a new dictionary and grammar book. Others began teaching the language at the Muckleshoot, Tulalip, and Swinomish Reservations. Being around Vi inspired us to volunteer for tasks we might previously have thought beyond our capability. If Vi believed us capable, then it was so.

Vi called us her Lushootseed family and brought us again and again to her home, especially on her birthday in July. She fed us salmon cooked by fire, each fillet pierced by a skewer of ironwood driven into the ground in front of the fire. In this method, the salmon is positioned vertically and the skewer (called a "fish stick") is turned once so that both sides of the fish cook to perfection. When we had eaten and visited in her huge backyard, at tables or on grass, there always came that moment when Vi stood. She thanked us for coming and then invited us one by one to stand and address the gathering. This was not an invitation we could refuse. When she called our names, we came to stand beside her and express our gratefulness to be right there, at the center of the world. Lushootseed projects were birthed at these gatherings, stories adopted, pregnancies announced, confessions made. Mumblers spoke clearly and the timid spoke with eloquence. It was our chance to make promises before witnesses we knew would support us in our endeavors, even hold us accountable. And always, the old words were spoken, a story told. ʔal tudiʔ tuhakʷ (A long time ago . . .)

ᘔ|ᖨ

Vi crossed into her eighties. Thick eyeglasses helped only a little with her vision loss. Her steps were smaller and she often took someone's arm. "I'm ancient," she told us—somehow skipping ever being old—and her link to the language, stories, and traditions of Lushootseed granted her that claim. She moved from Seattle up to "Skagit Country" near her birthplace. Her dining table moved with her.

She gathered us around her and spoke Lushootseed, while we scrambled to learn as much as we could. We knew that Vi had more to tell us. A former student named Zalmai "Zeke" Zahir decided to do the Grandmother Video Project with Vi, for which he asked her questions in Lushootseed about traveling by water, the language of the First People, the importance of stories, and Lushootseed life. Because Zeke asked her questions she had never been asked, she referred to it as "pushing the buttons." She responded to that button pushing at length in Lushootseed and later, when she watched the videotape, told us she was surprised at "what that old Indian lady inside me knows." She liked being surprised.

Vi and I recorded our conversations. I listened as she pulled up a memory of living up and down the Skagit River or how it happened that her parents entered into the longhouse tradition. Her talk sometimes journeyed further, paddling up the river of memory. But eventually her story looped around to the present because Vi knew how to bring things home. Following along behind her, I gathered her words as if they were blackberries. I placed them in a basket, careful not to let the jewels of this rich fruit slip through my fingers. There is work yet to be done in this place where the language lives.

Vi Hilbert and Janet Yoder (photo by Robby Rudine)

TEN THINGS
I LEARNED FROM
VI HILBERT

Vi Hilbert was a mentor to many people. Here are ten things I learned from her.

1. Make Strong Coffee

Every day Vi made pots of triple-strength French-roast coffee. She poured it into a big thermos that lived on her kitchen counter. She offered coffee to everyone who walked through her door. Vi's coffee fueled her work on Lushootseed, as well as her helpers: linguists, anthropologists, archaeologists, writers, composers, teachers, filmmakers, family, and friends. You drank Vi's coffee and you got wired on the sublime blend of being with Vi and doing the work. Magic and caffeine.

2. Fill Your Calendar

Vi was happiest when her calendar had lots of entries on it, when she had not one but two or three events a day: Zeke Zahir and Jay Miller coming to work on place names, Vi giving a talk to grade school teachers, then dinner with the Storytellers Guild. When I came to visit, Vi would hold out her calendar and ask, "Can you join me for any of this?" Her calendar marked her anticipated pleasure of being with people she loved or people she might come to love, of representing her culture, of doing her right work.

3. Live in Indian Time

My iPhone calendar has me select the start time and duration of anything I schedule. The default setting is one hour. Vi Hilbert's calendar only needed a start time, and she always arrived before the start time. It was a given that she would take Indian Time (a term she loved and used often) whenever she gathered with the people she loved. Vi's events lasted long enough for her to speak her heart, for others to speak their hearts, for some work, food, and strong coffee. Indian Time is shimmery. It expands to accommodate need, so you can pick mountain blackberries until you have enough to make jam that will last through the winter. Or to smoke salmon just pulled from the Skagit River. In Vi's world, Indian Time is generous, longed for, savored, and remembered.

4. Find Your Right Work

Your right work is a gift. Vi's ancestors guided her to her right work—her Lushootseed work—as if they knew all along and were just waiting for her to know. Vi guided others to find their right work: a book, a play, a musical, a map, a documentary, a children's show, a canoe program, teaching. Your right work will keep you energized, active, and in the world. Your right work will keep you connected to others doing their right work, perhaps keep you connected to your ancestors, perhaps even to the Creator.

5. Honor Your Ancestors

Vi honored her parents and her aunt Susie, a superb oral historian and healer, and all of her ancestors in the spirit world. She received their guidance daily at the altar in her living room, and at night through dreams or songs. Vi knew that when a message came to her, it was her ancestors speaking. She listened to their messages and let herself be guided by them. She knew that if she did not, she could become gravely ill. Or never again receive such a message. Vi knew each message from her ancestors was a gift that required her attention and respect.

6. Claim People

Vi called us her Lushootseed family. Whenever she left a message on our answering machine, she always began, "Hello, family." Vi called me *daughter* a few times. I know she said this as an endearment or acknowledgment. I know I am not her daughter. I am the daughter of my own fine mother. Still, I strive to live up to Vi's claim.

7. Be siʔab (See-AHB)

siʔab means "respected one," "honored one," or "treasured one." *siʔab* also means "noble" or "high-class," which refers to the people you come from as well as your behavior. Vi modeled how to be *siʔab*. She addressed everyone in her world as *siʔab* whenever she spoke. She set her expectation this way. You needed to behave in a *siʔab* way to be invited into Vi's world. You needed to become *siʔab*, or as close to it as you could get, if you wanted to stay there.

8. Be Frivolous

"I am going to be frivolous," Vi would announce. That meant having fun, going shopping at Nubia's for a lovely cape or a cashmere sweater. Or dinner at the top of the Space Needle, Anthony's, or The Brooklyn. Or finding the perfect long black skirt and leather boots to wear in the longhouse. Being frivolous meant Vi was stepping outside her role as cultural icon, elder, teacher, wise one, as the voice of Lushootseed. She would treat those being frivolous with her to a meal and perhaps a pair of earrings, thus being *siʔab* even while being frivolous.

9. Don't Worry about Money

Vi never worried about money. Not the money she lived on, not the money she needed for her projects, and not the money she gave to someone in her world who might need it. She did not worry about having enough money to last to the end of her life. She had better ways to expend her energies: commission a symphony inspired by spirit songs, make a documentary, gather the words of the ancestors into books, share those books with the world. The money would be there when needed.

10. Consider Danger as a Gift

In the early 1970s and again in 1985, Vi suffered a stroke. In 1985, she had surgery for an aneurism. After an arduous recovery, Vi approached her Lushootseed work with renewed commitment. She gave it her all, pushed to get everything done. She transcribed and translated recordings, worked on a new dictionary, a book of place names. She published books of her material, and she distributed them herself in all her travels around Indian Country and beyond. Her work came into a tight, sharp focus. Through both of her strokes and through her recovery from them, she got close enough to shake hands with death, and she took that meeting as a push to do her work.

Robby Rudine, Janet Yoder, Vi Hilbert, and Jay Miller at the Kāʻanapali Beach Hotel (photo courtesy Robby Rudine)

VI HILBERT
AND THE GIFT OF
LUSHOOTSEED

(This essay tells the story of Vi Hilbert's life and work, woven into a journey with her to the Longhouse at Tulalip for Treaty Day. She chose a few of her volunteers to invite to the longhouse to observe the traditions of the Treaty Day gathering each year. We knew this was not open to the public and that we were privileged to be there. I wrote "Vi Hilbert and the Gift of Lushootseed" [then titled "Vi's Lucid Years"] during her life, under her direction, and with respect for her rich cultural traditions. She read it and gave it her blessing. Then she made copies to give to family and friends, the best compliment a writer could receive.)

Vi Hilbert stands in her doorway, arms open. *həd?iw̓ b. həd?iw̓ b ti.* (Come in. Come in, you folks.) She speaks Lushootseed to welcome us. We answer as she taught us to do years ago in her language class. As an Upper Skagit elder, Vi has kept alive the language, stories, and teachings of her people. Lushootseed was the first language Vi heard as an infant. Her parents spoke it to each other at home. There are some who say Vi Hilbert is single-handedly responsible for preserving the Lushootseed language. She denies that and immediately credits other elders who speak the language, linguists, and all of her helpers, but no one can imagine the work getting done without her.

We've traveled western Washington's flat Skagit farmland under a shawl of winter cloud to Vi's new home at Bow, just below the Chuckanut Mountains. She has invited us to accompany her to the Tulalip Reservation for Treaty Day, the largest gathering of longhouse people. Vi pulls us each in for a kiss and hug and I must bend to embrace her. It's like holding a hummingbird between my hands. She feels tiny, energetic, fragile, and capable of hovering above her world while taking it all in. Vi used to cut hair professionally and keeps hers trimmed short. Her face is small behind her eyeglasses, giving her the look of a wise child. Her voice is like a sprinkle of rain, the kind of voice that makes you want to listen.

It's our first visit to Vi's new house. In her living room, tightly woven baskets and cedar bark dolls sit on her shelves as if they had always lived here, though only a short time ago they lived at her house on Des Moines Way South in Seattle. Carved cedar paintings by her son Ron Hilbert hang on the walls, each a view into the longhouse where dancers circle the fires, helpers all around them. He also painted a portrait on cedar of Vi and Don, to mark fifty years of a sometimes-bumpy marriage. The marriage is now nearly sixty, and the bumps have grown larger. Vi's Indian Shaker Church altar (carved by her father), with its white cloth, wooden cross, and candles, stands in front of the largest window, consecrating the interior with the land around it. "The spirit speaks to me here." Though Vi has lived here only two months, already her house feels familiar and inviting.

In each room, my eyes search out signs of Vi. Her necklaces, ones I've seen her wear many times, hang from hooks. I see big beads of amber, turquoise, ebony, and dentalium, awaiting selection. Her computer sits near her bed, like emergency gear, ready for the call to work. "I've moved the Brain Room in here." Her arm sweeps across the shelves of notebooks, videotapes, and audiotapes, testament to her work on Lushootseed.

We settle at her big, all-leaves-always-in dining table, the table where everything happens. The chairs swivel. Mine rocks slightly as I turn to face Vi at the head of the table. She pulls out her calendar and hands it to me. "See what's coming up. Maybe you can join me for some of these." Scratchy handwriting fills in the squares: a memorial service for Lummi leader Kenny Cooper, who shared a traditional name with Vi's son Ron; a naming for the favorite grandson of her cousin Dobie. Speaking gigs: one at Squaxin to dedicate a new hotel with a casino; another at the Eagle Festival on the Upper Skagit River. Her driver's name appears below each entry. Some squares show scholars who are coming to work with her on place names or stories, or to review her archive. "On my slow days, I'm going over my old materials." She points to an overstuffed chair by the fireplace and a table covered with books she has published in both Lushootseed and English, the recorded words of her ancestors.

Two years ago, Vi Hilbert announced she had ten lucid years left. We were sitting outdoors at a beer garden in Bellingham, Washington, after the close of the Salish Conference, a gathering of linguists who work with the Salish languages and of people who teach those languages in tribal settings. "So I'd better get busy. There is work yet to do." Her words were sure. I sat beside her on a bench and turned to see her calm face, eyes clear and definite. I remind myself that Vi has already completed eighty-five years, and it requires great lucidity to inhabit her world. "Now I'm asking the spirit, *What do I have left to do?* and I'm about to get a message." When she gets it, we will all know.

I glance at her calendar. Half the squares are full, and everything is written large. Even with her thick glasses, she can't see much. Macular degeneration has taken most of her sight. "I'm blind, dear," she told me matter-of-factly, once she accepted that her sight was not returning. She sees a little and gets around a lot. She keeps track of the people in her world on index cards, names and numbers printed large with her wide-tipped Magic Marker, one per card. It is her loose-leaf Rolodex. Seeing our card in the deck lifts my spirits.

As we leave for Tulalip, Vi takes my arm and we make our way to the car. Robby carries her longhouse supplies in a canvas bag: a large red blanket, bottles of water, Werther's butterscotch candies, and an envelope with money she might need to give to different people as the spirit moves her. Her father's drum—named Captain—with Eagle spreading his wings across the deerskin head, travels with us to Tulalip. Most important, she is bringing Lushootseed to the gathering.

⊐⌐

Vi was born to Charlie and Louise Anderson near the town of Lyman on the Skagit River on July 24, 1918. She grew up hearing Lushootseed and knowing the Skagit River as home. "We lived up and down the river," she said. "Wherever my dad could find work, that's where we lived. It might have been a garage or a chicken house, but my mother made it a home. She had a piece of linoleum that she put on the floor wherever we lived. If the walls were unbearable, she would wallpaper them, even if the wallpaper was newspaper." In the last decade of Vi's life, a house in Lyman came on the market. Since it was where Vi was born, I asked her whether she had any desire to buy it. "No," she said. "Lyman is just one place on the river."

⊐⌐

We drive south to Tulalip, a reservation thirty-five miles north of Seattle. With her failing vision, Vi now judges where she is by the rise and fall of the land, letting her internal GPS blend memory with topography. Near Tulalip, we turn off the freeway to travel west on Highway 528. It's dark now, and rain blurs the road signs. "We don't turn until the road goes downhill," Vi says. "I remember that hill from when my folks would bring me to the boarding school here. Going down that hill made me start crying. There was nothing wrong with boarding school, but saying goodbye to my folks broke my heart."

We make our way down to Mission Beach and arrive at the longhouse. Robby drops us near the door, then goes to park. Vi takes my arm, and we approach the big doors. A man stands in front, bulky in a thick Cowichan sweater. Tiny drops of rain nest in the weave like jewels. His arms cross his chest to add mass to his presence. "Hello, Vi." He nods, then opens the door attached to the house by giant hinges, and we pass through.

The sting of burning cedar. My eyes go to the fires. Sparks and smoke rise up to roof holes above to mix with the rain. The flames are the only light. Men move around each fire, tending them, building them up like Lincoln Logs with alternating layers of cedar and fire.

"Where do you want to sit?" our greeter asks.

"With the Upper Skagits," Vi says. He guides her to that section, and I follow. We wait under the Upper Skagit sign, with its crossed canoe paddles, while the man goes to get a chair to place on the longhouse earth floor in front of the bleacher seats. I cover the chair with the wool blanket and wrap a thick shawl around Vi's shoulders. She settles in like a plover fluffing herself into her winter nest. Robby joins me to climb up to the visitor row at the back of the bleachers.

We take our seats. For a moment, it feels like we are all painted into the grain of Ron Hilbert's carved cedar paintings. The longhouse feels smaller than on our previous visits, with more people squeezed within its walls. Dancers come with their helpers, as they have done each winter since their initiation. Vi has told us how each new dancer goes through a vigorous initiation—fasting, bathing in a cold stream, praying, seeking their *sqəlalitut*, their spirit power. Their cries and moans rise above the snap of the fire feeding on dry cedar. I hear what sounds like the call of a raven or the throaty growl of a bear, or the wail of childbirth. This is the warm-up, so everything goes on at once. Helpers support a dancer, with body, drumming, and song. No one does it alone. Though my eyes adjust to the firelight, I am never completely sure of what I am witnessing, only that it pounds in my chest, raw and strong.

Vi sits in her chair up front, as if she is in her own living room. People stop to greet her. She receives hugs and handshakes. She receives a kiss from her son Ron. Most likely she is the oldest person in the house, the one who links the tradition back to when her parents brought her to the longhouse. Tonight she will address those gathered here in the language her parents spoke.

ᘔ⎮ᖸ

Vi never entered the longhouse tradition where initiates seek and practice their spirit power, nor did she enter the healing tradition. "Even though I come from a long line of healers and medicine people, my dad said to me, *No, I'm not going to let you do that. You've got important work that you are going to do.*"

Vi did not set out to do Lushootseed work, though her early life certainly trained her for it. Not only did she hear the language from infancy, but she heard it used in different ways, from formal longhouse speech to teasing and sharing between her parents, who told each other their dreams each morning. "Visiting was a practice among my parents and their friends and relatives. It was not always in response to an invitation. You went to visit your friends and relatives when you got lonesome for them. It was a joyous feeling to hear a car drive in and turn off the engine or see a canoe pull up to the riverbank. Always I sat with the elders to listen to their exchanges in our ancient language."

Vi's parents tried to have many children. Of perhaps six pregnancies (and some births), only Vi survived. When she was young, Vi lamented having no brothers or sisters. But being an only child meant she paid closer attention to what her parents and their friends and relatives were saying. When she tried to answer them in Lushootseed, her parents laughed. "But I knew it pleased them. It delighted them. My parents heard from the authorities that children were to speak English, and so they expected me to do that. But sometimes I wanted to speak their language."

Vi attended fifteen different schools, as her folks moved up and down the Skagit River. Her dad did logging work, and both her parents picked strawberries, raspberries, and blackberries. When they sought work picking apples or hops across the Cascade Mountains in Yakima, they took Vi to the boarding school at Tulalip. During high school, she chose to attend the Chemawa Indian Boarding School in Oregon. Then she left Chemawa to work as a domestic in Portland so that she could go to public high school to achieve higher academic goals and integrate herself into a broader society. She graduated from Franklin High School in Portland, Oregon, in 1936. Through all Vi's schooling and moving around, Lushootseed stayed with her.

Vi's school friend Oma Woodcock introduced Vi to her brother. Vi married Percy Woodcock in 1936 and lived with him at his home in Taholah at the Quinault Reservation on the Olympic Peninsula. Their son, Denny, was born in 1937 and daughter, Lois, in 1938. During those years, Vi worked first at Indian Pete's Pool Hall and then in her very own café. "I had my carpenter husband build me a café where there was lots of room for visiting," Vi recounts. "I had a jukebox, pinball machines, slot machines, a marble soda fountain, plus a serve-yourself gas and oil business for all of the fishermen. I worked around the clock, lying down on the floor for a few winks, then getting back to work. I had a babysitter for my kids, but my lonely mother finally insisted that her grandchildren should come home to her at Nooksack while I was so busy. I let them go. My son became ill with meningitis, and at age three and a half, he died." After her son's death, her marriage to Percy and her life in Taholah came to a close. Vi and Lois joined her parents in their home at Everson in Nooksack Country north of Bellingham. During this time, she worked in a pear cannery in Everson, then in a café in Bellingham.

After some time, Vi went to Tulalip to visit her cousin Lillian, who introduced Vi to Bob Coy. Vi had first met Bob Coy when they were children at the Tulalip Boarding School. Their families knew each other. Vi was drawn to this handsome, smooth-dancing man from an important family. Vi married Bob Coy at Tulalip in 1942. They lived in Seattle, where Vi gave birth to Ron in 1943.

ᚠᛁᚠ

"The Tulalips are going to welcome you with their First Salmon Song," the floor manager says. Ron, now over sixty years old but still Hollywood-handsome, rises to gather with the others outside. They proceed into this house of cedar and begin their journey around the fires. They sing in Lushootseed, "Welcome, welcome, King Salmon. We honor you." They play drums held in the left hand, struck with beaters gripped in the right. The song is slow, a calm heartbeat. A song for King Salmon. Ron passes in front of us, singing. This is his first winter back in the house after hard years away. "Ron is traditional," Vi says. "He could have lived a hundred years ago. Maybe longer."

ᚠᛁᚠ

When her marriage to Bob Coy ended, Vi had two children to support. She found work as a stock clerk in a grocery store, then as a package wrapper in a Danish cookie bakery. "I wrapped hundreds of fancy boxes of Danish butter cookies," she says. During World War II, women were called on to do what had been men's work. In the spirit of Rosie the Riveter, Vi had only two weeks' training to become a skilled electrical welder on battleships for the war effort at Todd Pacific Shipyards in Tacoma. Hauling heavy equipment, Vi would climb a tall ladder to weld plates of metal that formed the sides of ships. Being tiny and with a precise touch, she also worked in the bowels of the ships. Vi took pride in this work. When peace brought an end to that challenging and lucrative job, she waited tables at a Chinese restaurant in South Tacoma.

Vi married Navy man Don Hilbert—her German American husband—in 1945. They lived in Seattle, where Vi worked as a cashier on the food wagon at Boeing, taking the swing shift so she could be home with her kids during the day and Don could be with them at night. She enrolled in Railroad School in Seattle to learn railroad telegraphy, secretarial skills, and the use of office machines. Vi concentrated on secretarial skills, which led to the job of secretary to the director of nursing at Children's Orthopedic Hospital. "It was wonderful work. I had lots of responsibility (including giving comfort to Native children) and was surrounded by dedicated, professional people. It was still not exactly what I needed to do with my life. I quit and went back to school, this time beauty school. After graduating, I worked for two salons in order to qualify for my own license. Then I opened a hair-bending salon out of my home that was so popular I was able to select clientele for the next ten years."

ᓚᔑᓓ

Now the longhouse floor manager summons six guests of honor to take seats up front, to speak to the house. "We'd like to ask *taqʷšəblu* to come forward, please." One of the men escorts Vi to sit with the other five speakers.

The floor manager calls on them one by one. Each of them speaks, eloquently welcoming all the guests to the house. "I want to thank each and every one of you who are here tonight," one man says. "You are here for a reason. We are observing our right to practice our religion here. That's what Treaty Day is about. We are keeping our culture alive, and our language." But he doesn't address us in Lushootseed. Nor do the others.

When her turn comes, Vi stands and walks forward in small steps, letting her feet search for a hold on the earth floor. She looks tiny, even frail. Those near her look ready to step up and offer their arms. But Vi gets her feet under her. A hush falls. Everyone knows her, knows that she can call up the old words and offer them here, a blessing on the house.

Vi speaks. Her soft voice makes us strain to listen. The old words are heard between the glottal stops, that tightening in the back of the throat that punctuates sounds, balanced by the lateral *ł* where air flows on either side of the tongue to make a leaky hiss. Vi doesn't rush. She lets the words live in the air, like released birds that hover before flying off to the sky. "*gʷəlapu siʔiʔab syəyaʔya čəł.* (My beloved people, all my noble relatives.)" Vi continues in Lushootseed. "I thank you for being here in this place, to do the important spirit work." Some faces nod in recognition of her words.

Now that Lushootseed has opened a door, she moves into English. Then, alternating languages, she tells the story of Treaty Day. "This is how it happened," she begins. "Charles Milton Buchanan was the big man back then, the Indian agent. He came here and said, *If you can show that you folks have something, then I will let you practice your religion.* So Elzie Andrews, my relation from Upper Skagit, sang his *sqəlalitut*, his spirit power. It was Cougar. When he did that, a cougar appeared and walked into the house. The Indian agent saw that cougar, and he was afraid. *Okay, okay, you folks have shown me. Now just make it go away!*" Vi looks around and nods at all the dancers, their helpers, and witnesses. "So we know we do indeed have something that we practice here at Treaty Day."

I listen, as I did in Vi's classroom. My ears reach for the words. I catch one, like catching a salmon in a dip net. I lift this sacred fish into the air where its silver scales flash in the sunlight. After a few seconds, the salmon surges out of the net to return to the river. It flips its tail and travels up, against the flow. Survival requires more than just the salmon, even a King Salmon. It calls for the river as well, the place Vi was born.

Her words float over the firepits, mixing with smoke and spreading to the four corners of the house, before rising up and out the smoke holes to the sky.

⊓⌐

Once I asked Vi who will speak Lushootseed at traditional gatherings when she no longer does. She hesitated, then named a couple of people. She said they may have gaps but they will step up.

"I have gaps, too," Vi tells me.

"But you find the words, *tsi si?ab*," I remind her. "Your resources are deep."

"I have no choice but to speak. I didn't always have the courage to do that. I never spoke it in public while my folks were alive."

"But you speak it as well as they did," I insist.

"No, dear," she says. "I don't. But I have to speak it. Then while I'm speaking, I find a few people who know the language. They won't stand and speak it. They are afraid of making a mistake. But they know it, some of it. So I talk to them. And I talk to my folks and all my relatives who are on the other side."

Vi talks about the other side as if it is right here, just around a corner in the house or up into the Chuckanut Mountains. Or through the fire. "I see and hear those people," she says. "That makes some people disturbed. But the ones on the other side give me encouragement." And Vi passes on her own encouragement from this side. New ones rise up to learn and eventually to speak, when there is no longer anyone above them. Vi is speaking to them, to the future.

⊐∥⊏

Vi continues addressing the longhouse, layering languages into a sandwich where Lushootseed is the meaty center and English the bread. "My dad said, *Say your piece and then sit down.* So I'm going to stop now. I want to thank the Tulalips for inviting me to speak here tonight. I thank all you dear ones." She sits. I feel sorry for the speaker that follows her. Indeed, the next one's words sound incomplete, as if they were sent out too early, like cookies whose centers are still raw. Vi gives the full meal, where listeners know they have truly feasted.

⊐∥⊏

Vi's Lushootseed wake-up call came in 1967. Linguist Thomas Hess had been working on the language with Nooksack elder Louise George for a number of years in her Seattle home. When they began work on a recording of Vi's mother telling the Basket Ogress story in Lushootseed, Louise told Thom he should call Vi, who lived nearby and ran a hair salon in her home. Vi came to Louise's home to, as Thom put it, "look into this white kid who was writing down in Lushootseed one of her own mother's stories." Vi's interest was caught, first by the fact that Thom could pronounce her name *taqʷšəblu* correctly and second by the writing system. Thom said, "She seemed intrigued by the fact that there was a system for spelling the language, which had a symbol for every sound; and she was definitely interested when I told her that she could learn to read and write it in a month or less, which she later did. By the end of that session, it was arranged that Vi would come to our next meeting and begin to learn to read and write Lushootseed."

The University of Washington invited Thom Hess to teach a class about Salish languages, specifically Lushootseed, in 1972. As he recalls, "Vi attended every class. She sat in the front row and made it a success in several ways, the most important of which was by assuring the students that the words that white man was saying were indeed Lushootseed." Thom was asked to teach the class again but had other commitments in British Columbia. So he arranged with the Indian studies department for Vi to teach the class. He talked long and hard to get her to agree. "She was reluctant in the beginning but felt a strong sense of obligation to do it in memory of her people and for the need of Native young people." Vi went to work. She and Thom wrote lesson plans for daily classes, a textbook, and later a dictionary. Then came the first *Haboo* book, traditional stories written down as they had been told.

Then Vi went to work on the Metcalf tape recordings. Like spindle whorls, these tapes allowed Vi to spin Lushootseed material as rich as mountain goat wool. Leon Metcalf had grown up partly among Tulalips, from whom he'd heard and learned some Lushootseed, especially while working in logging and at a wood mill. Later he taught music at a college in Seattle in the early 1950s. He remembered the elders he had known and feared the loss of information as those eloquent Lushootseed speakers grew close to the end of their lives. So, with his own time and money, he traveled around Indian Country carrying some of the earliest, bulky reel-to-reel tape-recording equipment. He sought out and recorded the most fluent speakers with the greatest wealth of stories, history, and memories. He played recordings of one elder for another as a means of triggering memory. He came to realize that these elders had known each other when they were young, but now lived some distance from each other and could no longer travel to visit in person. So Metcalf recorded their personal messages to each other and delivered them on his rounds, making him the mailman for this oral culture. Vi's aunt Susie Sampson Peter was one of these elders.

Since Aunt Susie did not have electricity, that first session was recorded in another home. By the time Metcalf returned for the next session, Aunt Susie had electricity in her house. She was ready to work. Years later, when the Metcalf tapes came into Vi's hands, she, too, was ready to work.

"I listened to a few words, then stopped the tape and wrote those words down. If I didn't understand something, I left a blank. Sometimes there were lots of blanks. Then I rewound and listened again, then again, and again. Maybe I could fill in a blank." Vi worked her way through the tapes, writing down in Lushootseed what she could, then translating into English. Her husband, Don, drove her in their camper out in search of elders and kin, like Dewey Mitchell, Martin Sampson, Martha Lamont, and Helen Ross, who could help her decipher speech and answer questions about grammar and shades of meaning. They might stay there for days while Vi asked all of her questions. Vi filled notebook after notebook with her handwritten Lushootseed. Back at home, she typed up everything she had managed to transcribe on an IBM Selectric typewriter with a specialized typeball that held the orthography based on the International Phonetic Alphabet. Later she input everything in Lushootseed into the linguistically capable but complex Terak computer, where it could be saved, edited, and printed.

As Thom Hess described it, "I do not believe anyone can fully appreciate what Vi has accomplished with those Metcalf tapes. First of all, there are lots of them. Second, very many of them are in poor quality so that they are difficult to hear—sometimes well-nigh impossible. Third, the people recorded spoke sophisticated Lushootseed with lots of words unknown today. With all this, Vi grappled indefatigably, listening over and over and over again. She scoured the entire region, seeking out the best remaining speakers to listen to this and that passage in hopes that still more might be gleaned. No one else could have done this work, and almost no one would have been willing to. Thanks to her herculean efforts, much more history, grammar, lexicon, and myth have been saved from oblivion than posterity had any right to expect. Only she knows at what effort this has been done."

But when I ask Vi about the effort, she tells me, "That work was a gift. *sxᵂit'il sʔuyayus*. Work that the Creator bestowed on me. I was ordained to do this work. It was always there, waiting for me to do."

Over time, Vi's ordained work received recognition. In 1989, she was named a Washington State Living Treasure. Then in 1994, she received a National Heritage Fellowship from the National Endowment for the Arts in Washington, DC.

꘎

Vi is brought back to her seat at the edge of the earth floor in the Upper Skagit section of the longhouse. Now the spirit dancing begins in earnest. The first dancer makes his way down the floor, surrounded by many helpers. They fill the house with his song. They beat on drums with padded sticks that bounce off the skin, again, again, again. This is a spirit power song. We stand to honor this ancient song and this young dancer passing in front of us. Vi raises her hands in welcome.

After a while, another dancer passes. Time brushes by in the opposite direction. All of it right in front of Vi.

꘎

Vi has recordings of her father singing spirit songs. Although she insists that she cannot sing them herself, she will sometimes

choose to pass a song on. "My dad sang over one hundred beautiful spirit songs that come from the ancestors of many of the
younger generation who are now singing in the longhouses.
As I observe them and listen to them, I will say to the younger
ones who are doing a good job with their involvement in the
longhouse or the Indian Shaker Church, *Have you been able to
hear your grandfather's song? Have you been able to hear your
grandmother's song?** *No*, they say. *Well, I see how you're handling yourself. Would you like to have a. copy of the way your
grandmother, your grandfather, your uncle, your relative sang
this same song?* If they indicate they would be pleased to have
that, then I will make them a copy and make them a gift of it."

Not everyone welcomes Vi's offer. "Sometimes, some of those
people who have become members of the longhouse feel very upset
that their ancestor's song has been sung by my dad and recorded.
I've offered them a copy of it. But they just get all tied up in knots.
And I say, *I didn't mean to hurt you. I meant to make you a gift of
something that you might cherish. No, no*, they say. *We don't like
what you're doing. We don't like what you're doing.* Then many
years later, they say, *May we have a copy of our grandmother's
song?* I say, *I offered it to you once. You mean you want it now?
Yes.* They've become established in their work, and they realize
how important that gift is. Now they can receive it."

Vi maintains the long view, that her work is valuable, and in
time, people will come to appreciate it. She is sometimes harshly

---

*The Indian Shaker Church is not related to the Shaker Church of New
England. The Indian Shaker Church was founded by a couple at Mud
Bay, near Olympia, in 1881 when a Squaxin healer named John Slocum
came back from the dead with the mission of starting a new religion. His
wife, Mary, trembled and shook, at first in grief, then in prayer, especially
healing prayer. Many Indian Shaker Church songs are sung at gatherings
throughout Puget Sound Indian Country as well as in the Indian Shaker
Church services. Many converts to the Indian Shaker Church also convert
their longhouse songs to their new religion at the same time.

criticized in Indian Country for making material available. Like a canoe captain, Vi keeps an eye on the horizon, not just the roil around the boat. Every captain needs paddlers to help pull the canoe through the water. Vi has many who pull with her, from Indian Country and beyond: storytellers, archivists, linguists, anthropologists, teachers, filmmakers, editors, and writers. Vi doesn't ask people to help with the work. She believes the right people will always step up.

In my first class with Vi, she welcomed us in a soft voice, as if telling us secrets that we suddenly longed to know. "Now each of you will tell me who you are." One by one we introduced ourselves, tribal people naming their affiliation, the rest of us naming the place we were born, along with a recipe for our personal melting pot.

Then she put up a drawing of the river with cedars and firs on either side and salmon leaping up into a perfect arc above the water. "The animals lived there," Vi said. And her voice told us it had always been so. *stuləkʷ*, we learned, was river. *sʔuladxʷ* was salmon. *yəx̌ʷəlaʔ* was eagle, and *spaʔc* was bear. We worked our way around the circle of animals, a cast of characters. We would come to know them as we did our own family's quirky uncle who plays silly tricks on everyone, then laughs uproariously, or an aunt always worrying about danger.

So it began. Our daily visit to the world of Lushootseed. There were a dozen of us who passed through that door. Vi welcomed us each time and thanked us at the end of every class, as if we had given her something. It made me want to give her something. We greeted each other in the language, asked how the other was. We asked about families, ages, how many years we had lived here in Seattle. We spoke of our dogs and cats, whose stories joined those of the animals who were people.

Over the years, Vi inspired many of us to continue our Lushootseed work, to take on tasks, even large ones. When

I asked her how she managed to do this, she said, "The spirit chooses the responsible people."

We knew we were accepted when Vi invited us to her birthday party, in the sloping backyard of her house on Des Moines Way in South Seattle, just above Boeing Field and not far from the mythic site on the Duwamish River where South Wind battled North Wind. We gathered each July to feast on salmon staked on ironwood skewers carved by her husband, Don, and cooked in front of the fire her son and husband tended with expert care. Vi made scalloped potatoes; her daughter, Lois, baked at least a hundred individual tarts, filled with berries, pecans, and chocolate or lemon pudding, all topped with whipped cream. Guests brought their own traditional food—southern fried chicken, fry bread with homemade blackberry jam, nettle soup, or crunchy herring roe on kelp brought by visitors from Alaska, even sushi made by a Japanese guest.

Academics and tribal folks mingled with Vi and Don's square-dancing buddies, all of us swinging past the food table to admire its bounty that increased with each new arrival. Vi always called on a Lushootseed speaker to ask the blessing.

Eating was good. And never rushed. Vi gave us the time we needed to weave our connections. Each year produced a different basket. There were always some surprise guests: a young filmmaker she had met, a mythologist seeking entry into story time, or a neighbor who had just moved here from Thailand. We filled ourselves on salmon straight from the fire. We visited until Vi gave the signal. Then we fell silent.

Vi stood. She spoke in Lushootseed, and those of us who had studied it, no matter how many years it had been, recognized certain words: *thank you, dear ones, good food, salmon, family, home, heart, place,* and *people.* I imagined those same words being spoken here hundreds of years ago, or a thousand. Then she gave most of her message again in English, where the words sounded slimmer, as if Coyote or Bear had taken a bite out of the flesh, leaving only bones and skin. She thanked us for blessing her home, her world. Then she began to call on us.

You stand when Vi calls your name. You step forward to embrace her and then stand beside her. No matter what you have prepared to say, you can surprise yourself, as if a Lushootseed spirit whispers in your ear. You might take on a huge task, one you had not planned on doing, a book or a documentary. Or you might find tears sliding down your cheek as you thank Vi for helping you through the loss of a parent or a child. You might share your hopes for the child you carry. You might sing the story of Humpy, that ugly old salmon who believes he is young and handsome as he travels upriver in search of all the pretty Salmon Women. You might make everyone laugh. Or cry. You might speak Lushootseed. Inevitably, you will help lift the spirit of everyone gathered and you will feel your spirit lift.

In Vi's backyard, we supped on these words as hungrily as we had eaten the food. The summer sky darkened. Vi thanked us all and closed the circle. Folks made their way home, carrying the courage to do what was next.

⊒∥⊏

Robby and I get the signal that Vi is ready to leave the longhouse. Since our arrival, more people have crowded into the bleachers between our seats and Vi's. With no aisles or railings, we need their cooperation. They stand and lift up the blankets from the benches so we can work our way down to Vi.

A dancer begins his journey down the floor just as we join Vi. We can't move until after he passes. So we stand and quietly mark rhythm to his song with our hands, knuckles to palms. The drums thunder, and my heart beats against my chest. He dances past us, followed by helpers to keep him from straying toward the fires or the edge of the house. I turn to Vi. She smiles as he passes, as if recognizing him, his song, or the spirit he carries. Or maybe she recognizes his ancestor who once danced in this way.

We step out of the longhouse. Vi says goodbye to a group of men outside the door. Then we are in the parking lot full of pickup trucks with fishing gear in the back, old sedans, new minivans, and SUVs. Rain falls lightly, idly. Drops land on my face, cooling the heat in my cheeks.

Before Robby can offer to get the car, Vi takes my arm and steps softly across the rainy mix of mud and gravel at our feet. She speeds toward the car, head high, feet sure, as if her own mountain goat power is moving through her. I think how each dancer has her helpers. No one does it alone. Helpers move all around each dancer to keep her from straying too close to the fire, to keep her on the earth floor where everything happens. We are fortunate to count ourselves among Vi's helpers, the ones on this side, in her Lushootseed journey.

Sheet of six stamps depicting Vi Hilbert (stamps by Robby Rudine)

Vi Hilbert standing between her parents, Charlie and Louise Anderson (photo courtesy Lushootseed Research)

Son Ron Hilbert in front of his paintings at Vi Hilbert's Seattle home
(photo courtesy Lushootseed Research)

Daughter Lois Dodson and Vi Hilbert at Upper Skagit
(photo courtesy Lushootseed Research)

Siblings Lois Dodson and Ron Hilbert (photo courtesy Lushootseed Research)

Thom Hess, Louise George, and Vi Hilbert (photo courtesy Lushootseed Research)

Leon Metcalf (photo courtesy Lushootseed Research)

Salmon drawing Vi Hilbert used in her Lushootseed class (drawing by Ron Hilbert)

Governor Booth Gardner naming Vi Hilbert a Washington State Living Treasure
(photo courtesy Lushootseed Research)

Vi Hilbert receiving a National Heritage Fellowship in Washington, DC
(photo courtesy Lushootseed Research)

Don Hilbert cooking salmon for the annual backyard gathering
(photo courtesy Lushootseed Research)

RIGHT WORK

Vi could have gone down the path of traditional healers. She could have become a traditional healer, like her most revered relatives, Susie Sampson Peter or Isadore Tom. She could have entered longhouse life, received her song, and danced her spirit dance. She could have gone into the Indian Shaker Church to become a spiritual leader. But Vi's father told her she was not to do any of that: "You have work that you will do, Daughter." So she resisted the callings, resisted the spirit songs that came to her, resisted the dreams that pulled her toward that world.

Instead she found her right work in Lushootseed. Vi believed that her father knew she would find it. "Bless his heart. He was so wise. He was preparing me from the time I was born to take my rightful place in the world, in the culture of our world. He prepared me by disciplining me to listen."

Vi admitted, "If it had not been for Thom Hess coming into my life, Lushootseed probably would have died right there. I wouldn't have known that I had the kind of memories that could be used for the Lushootseed work. He was patient to work with me. He never allowed me to feel that I was too dumb to learn.

"You know," she said, "before I ever worked with Thom, somewhere I picked up a book that had work by Erna Gunther about Salish peoples of western Washington State. I was delighted to find something written about my culture. So I think that the fact that something had been written was what allowed me to become interested in being involved in the first place. Because it was so exciting to see something written."

I asked Vi how she felt when she was first asked to teach Lushootseed. "I felt completely inadequate to the task. Then I got brave enough to try anyway because there was nobody else. I was it."

"What if you had not found this work?" I asked.

"Oh, how barren would my life have been, had I not had this important work to do, that continues to feed me in many emotional ways. I realize there is so much yet that I need to try to pass on while I'm here. The culture is so rich with things that need to be passed on. It's frustrating to me that I probably won't have time to do all the things I should do while I'm here. I felt that way while my elders were alive. I had a chance to work with them, but I didn't know what kind of questions to ask them, just as you are finding time to ask me questions. I didn't realize that I should be peppering them with questions that the future would need to hear about."

I asked Vi the taboo question, the question about asking questions. "So many of us were taught never to ask questions," she said. "That was part of what inhibited me from asking my parents questions. I heard from a very young age, *You are not to ask questions. You are never to ask questions.* That's a taboo thing. *If you have to ask questions,* my cousin Minnie said, *then it means that you were too dumb to learn by just listening.* But it's no longer that. It's that we don't have time to just listen until the answers come. So you have to ask questions to take a shortcut in the culture."

When Vi wanted to fill in the blanks on her transcription or ferret out multiple layers of meaning, she traveled into Indian Country to seek out elders who spoke Lushootseed. She broke the rule about asking questions. She asked questions out of her drive to preserve all the information for the future when there might be even fewer fluent speakers. "But," she said, "I wish I had asked my folks questions. Because now they are gone, and I can't go back and ask them.

"Questions are button pushers. If someone asks me something I have never been asked before, that question might push a button in my memory and out comes something I didn't know I knew. That's a gift. Somehow that brain the Creator gave to each one of us allows us to reclaim information whether we know we remember or not. It's in that gray matter that never ever goes on overload. It's amazing. It's always there."

Every time I interviewed Vi, when we finished, she always said, "Thank you for asking the questions."

Vi Hilbert Hall at Seattle University (photo by Robby Rudine, Vi Hilbert photo in hall by Paul Eubanks)

RIVER TALK

We launch. The Skagit River pulls gently on our inflated raft, inviting us further. It's winter in western Washington. Clouds blanket the mountains on either side of the river, squeezing a misty spray on our heads and bundled bodies. Around a bend, we sight our first eagle, one of many that we'll see. They've come to feed on spawned-out salmon. We've come to admire them. We've also come to be with Vi.

Eagles sit regally on the branches, watching us float by below. Vi calls up to them in Lushootseed, "*hiwiləx̌ saq̓ʷax̌ʷ* (Go and fly now)." They spread their wings, sweeping their way downriver to await our further admiration. Would the eagles have flown if Vi had asked in English? "I like to think it only works in Lushootseed," she says.

The ancient language carries across the water and up to the trees. Vi addresses some of the eagles as *wiw̓su* (babies) or *ləgʷəb* (teenagers), but there is no mistaking the *hikʷ siʔab yəx̌ʷlaʔ* (grand and most honored eagle). Completely white-headed, he sits on a lower branch so that we may admire his wise old face. Vi talks to him and then tells us, "He's saying, *Yes, I know I am beautiful. I am glad you are watching and I am glad you've come to visit me.*" The babies perch on higher branches, less sure of their floating visitors.

There is no doubt the language carries power. Vi speaks, and the sounds echo on the river of her birth. All of us in the raft have heard Vi speak Lushootseed many times, but it's different here on the river, where her ancestors have spoken the language for millennia.

We spy more eagles perched in a single tree. We turn our heads to keep them in view as our oarswoman, Andie Palmer, twirls us through an eddy. Likewise, the eagles turn their heads to follow our progress, and I wonder what they perceive of our bulging oblong doughnut raft and our eager, admiring faces.

What started as a sprinkle when we launched is now a serious rain, so we pull our hoods up over our knit hats and pass around cups of Vi's strong black coffee. The cold air and the coffee make us hungry. Sandwiches make their way around the raft, and then Vi's carrot cake. Andie drops her oars to eat, letting the current take us for a time.

After lunch, Vi requests a river song and one of our rafters obliges with a song of the Shenandoah, then another about barges on the Mississippi in the hot sun. In turn, we ask Vi for a Skagit River song. Instead of singing, Vi tells of going out on this river with her dad in a shovel-nose canoe that he poled rather than paddled. "He knew all the places where the fish were. He hummed his songs when he was going to one of those places to fish. He didn't sing real loud; he just hummed under his breath. In an eddy like that, he'd use his dip net. He would tie his canoe to a tree limb and very quietly pull his dip net through the water until he caught a salmon. Sometimes it took a long time to catch one, but he had lots of patience.

"But he could also use a spear. He knew where to go, to log-jams where he could get right out over the water. There would be places where he could see down through the clear water, and then

he could spear fish. He knew every inch of the river. He learned
it from his father.

"I was never allowed to touch any of his fishing things. That
was his territory. It was not for me. But I fished for trout with
a grocery string and a bent pin. There were lots of trout in the
Skagit, and if I had a string, a rock, and a willow pole, why, I
could catch fish. I used worms mainly because if we had salmon
eggs, we used those for eating, not for bait. Once in a while, my
mother let me have part of a skein of salmon eggs. Boy, those
worked great; I could really catch fish with those."

We float and I consider salmon. I recall being with Vi on
the Tulalip Reservation, where we watched fishermen catch the
first returning king salmon of the season and paddle it to shore
in a cedar dugout canoe. One fisherman lifts this first salmon
up above his head. King is the largest salmon—up to five feet
long and one hundred pounds. The people gather on the shore at
Tulalip Bay to welcome this salmon as if he were royalty. This
first salmon is placed on a bed of cedar branches and sword fern.
Two men carry the salmon up to the longhouse. The people sing
hikʷ siʔab yubəč ("Big Chief King Salmon") to honor this fish
and give thanks for his return. The first salmon, followed by
everyone gathered, leaves the longhouse. A fisherman cooks this
salmon and the honored fish is shared with honored guests, and
perhaps a bit of its flesh goes to the fire to feed the ancestors.
The fish skeleton—with head and tail still attached—is carried
back into the longhouse, followed by all of the people. Finally
the salmon skeleton is carried down to the beach, placed in the
canoe, and paddled out into Tulalip Bay, where he is returned to
the water. If this king salmon makes a good report on his treat-
ment to all his salmon relatives, then salmon will fill the water-
ways and feed the people.

Vi recalls her mother's own first salmon ceremony. "My
mother saw my father coming home with a big king salmon. She
grabbed that salmon and she kissed it, welcoming it. I still see

that picture in my mind. She honored the gift from the spirit. They never, ever took anything for granted. It was something they cherished. The king salmon, every part of it was wonderful."

We listen to Vi's stories as the river laps softly against our raft. She talks about the villages along the river's banks and I can almost see them. "People knew each other," she continues. "This was their highway."

Time seems to stop, or maybe flow backward as the river beckons us around the next bend. "Everything about the river was spirit help: the ripples in the water, the whirlpools, and the eddies. People would bathe in the river in winter when they were looking for their spirit help. It had to be unpolluted, clear, cold water. It's a discipline, and you have to have a mindset that says, *My body is going to endure this. I'm doing this for a special purpose.*"

The chill of a winter bath gets easier to imagine as the rain steadily increases. I realize that I have no feeling in my feet, and I notice Vi's hands are curled up inside her sweater. I confess to my frozen toes. "Tell your toes they aren't cold," Vi says. "That's what I'm telling my hands."

We are getting close to our take-out spot. I jump out with the rope and pull us in, wondering whether my feet will obey my command. I send a strong message down to them, with promises of warmth to come. Somehow they support me, and soon there's a helping hand from someone on shore.

We empty the raft of ourselves, our gear, and finally the water we have accumulated. We pack up the raft. Then we climb into Vi's camper for some most welcome heat, smoked salmon, apple slices, and hot coffee with a splash of Metaxa brandy.

We drive back to the city. At home, I put on a pot of tea, unlayer myself, and take a hot soak. In bed, I close my eyes and am back on the river. It lulls me with its whispery flow; I drift off to visions of eagles and voices from the past.

Eagles in a tree (photo by Paul Eubanks)

Vi with Andy Fernando on a different (and sunnier) visit to the Skagit River
(photo by Paul Eubanks)

Ron and Don Hilbert with fresh caught salmon
(photo courtesy Lushootseed Research)

THE OLD CANOE IS THE NEW CANOE

IN THE BEGINNING

In the beginning, the people traveled by canoe. "If we didn't have a canoe," Vi said, "we were just without transportation unless we walked somewhere. But the canoe could take us up and down the river in order to visit relatives. The river was our highway. We had a canoe to get us there."

In the beginning, the people traveled out to sea in solid, thick-hulled canoes. They traveled hundreds of miles across salt water from mainland to islands, the San Juans, Guemes, Lummi, and Utsalady on Camano Island. They traveled to and from Swinomish, S'Klallam, Suquamish, Musqueam, Saanich, Samish, anywhere a canoe could travel.

In the beginning, the people went fishing and hunting by canoe. In the Lushootseed-speaking world of Puget Sound, the collective term for canoe is q̓il̓bid (KALE-BEAD). If the people moved downriver to fish camp, they would travel in a ƛ̓əlay̓ (shovel-nose canoe). On the return trip upriver, this ƛ̓əlay̓ carried home their supply of salmon, herring, clams, mussels, oysters, and gooseneck barnacles. A hunter would take a *sdəxʷił* (hunting canoe), and in it he would bring back his catch: bufflehead ducks, mergansers, mallards, or in coastal areas perhaps a seal. At Makah, out on the northwestern tip of the Olympic Peninsula, hunters went out in a canoe to hunt whale. What can we say about the courage it took to hunt whale in a dugout canoe? In summer—the time of canoe races—the people gathered to test their strength, endurance, spirit power, and speed in a *x̌ix̌q̓wił* (racing canoe).

Consider this: Each time the people put a canoe into the water, there is danger. Storms, winds, waves, fog, chill. People set out and some of these people do not come back. Traveling by canoe is not a Sunday drive. Not then, not now. In the 2006 Canoe Journey, a sudden heavy wind in the Strait of Juan de Fuca capsized a canoe called *The Hummingbird*; Chief Jerry Jack of Mowachaht/Muchalaht of northern Vancouver Island drowned.

After death, an important person traveled between worlds in a canoe that held their body. This canoe was sent downriver toward the sea or placed on sturdy tree branches. You could spend your whole life in a canoe and travel to the next world in that same canoe.

CARVING THE RED CEDAR DUGOUT CANOE

Vi Hilbert's father, Charlie Anderson, carved canoes and was famous for his racing canoes. "I would watch him select a tree," Vi said. "I would say to him, *Dad, what kind of tree are you looking for?* His answer was *A female tree.* And I said, *Why a female tree?* He said, *Because the grain is different. It is stronger than the male tree.*" They say that a carver had to be able to hear the tree speak so he could choose the right tree, an old-growth tree, which means a Pacific red cedar anywhere from four hundred to eight hundred years old. A carver fasted and cleansed before choosing the tree. Word is the carver did not comb his hair during carving for fear of splitting the hull. He would also remain celibate during carving. He would give everything he had to the creation of his canoe.

It takes a village to carry the red cedar log—the future canoe—back to the village. If the log is near water, it can be floated back. In the water, the log will settle and reveal which side will be the top of the canoe.

The carver digs out the opening in the log. Before metal tools, he would have used elk horn, yew-wood wedges, bone, mussel shells, beaver incisors, jadeite, or nephrite to carve the sacred cedar tree. He would use fire to hollow out the opening. Now a canoe carver may use a maul, awl, ax, elbow adze, D-adze, or a crooked knife. Perhaps a chain saw for roughing out the log. But the D-adze will give the regular textured finish to the cedar, the finish we know from totem poles, house posts, and plank houses.

The carver spreads the canoe. He places hot stones inside the opening, then adds a few inches of water. He covers the opening with a cedar bark mat and waits for the steam to make the wood fiber flexible. Then he gently taps the wood to push out the sides and inserts a thwart to brace it crosswise and hold the opening.

Vi says her father learned to carve a canoe by watching. "It's a thing that you can't be taught. It has to be something that you observe. His hands were his teachers. He'd feel the wood and then carve accordingly. He was very intelligent about how the canoe would act on the water. The race canoe was thinner and had a way of skimming through the water, whereas the work canoe was heavier and had more body to it."

PADDLE TO SEATTLE, 1989

pədgʷədbixʷ, time of blackberries—July. You go to Shilshole, an ancient village site, now Golden Gardens Park in the city of Seattle. You have known Vi for eleven years, and she invites you to join her on this summer evening under a lambent sky on the edge of Puget Sound. You will later learn this is part of the Salish Sea. Today you will witness the return of Indian canoes. Pacific red cedar dugout canoes.

Washington State is now one hundred years old. In the lead-up to this centennial, the state and local tribes—under the leadership of Quinault elder Emmett Oliver—open the way for this canoe event to happen. Suquamish and Duwamish Tribes agree to host. Other tribes agree to help. The US Forest Service makes old-growth cedar trees available to Swinomish, Upper Skagit, Nooksack, and Lummi for canoes. A few master carvers come forward to teach. Canoes are carved. Canoe travel skills are practiced. Emmett Oliver coins the name: Paddle to Seattle.

People gather at the beach at Shilshole. Tribal people, some in cedar bark hats, headbands, and visors. Media people with big cameras. All kinds of people. All facing the water. You see eleven canoes in the distance, that long iconic shape, some with prows carved in the form of a dog head or deer head, so it appears that animal spirits guide these canoes.

Now the canoes converge and float side by side just off shore. A figure in an ermine headdress stands in the bow of one of the canoes and begins to dance. Her crew sings. In their native language, they announce who they are and where they are from, which in Indian Country amounts to the same thing. The dancer releases bird down into the air, and the breeze lifts these lightest of feathers as a blessing.

In each canoe, eleven paddlers (called *pullers*) hold their paddles at attention, with paddle ends straight up. One canoe captain greets the crowd on the beach. He asks in his language for permission for his canoe to come ashore.

The hosts grant permission—in Lushootseed—and the pullers paddle the canoe closer, then leap out and haul their canoe through the shallow water. People on shore walk into the water to help draw the canoe up onto the sandy beach. Everyone wants to touch the canoe, to affirm its presence among us. Someone places a wreath of cedar boughs over the prow. Each canoe arrives on the shore. Each canoe is welcomed as one welcomes a relative returning from far away. Because this is done in the language of each arriving canoe and in the language of the host, each arrival gives the language strength.

You turn to Vi and the people all around. You see a luminous pride. On this one evening, you know you are in the right place, at the center of this canoe world. The air smells of salt, smoke, salmon, fire, and cedar. You witness something that could have taken place a hundred years ago when Washington became a state, or even a thousand years before that.

RACING CANOES, STOMMISH

Lois Dodson (Vi's daughter), Ed (Lois's partner), Jay Miller, Robby, and I go with Vi to Stommish—the canoe races hosted by the Lummi Tribe on Hale Passage, which separates Lummi Island from the mainland near Bellingham, Washington. *Stommish* means "warrior" in Lummi. Racing canoes were known as war canoes because they are fast. Eleven warriors can make a racing canoe fly across the water at the speed of eleven knots. The warriors would race out from shore in those canoes when northern raiders approached in larger canoes, coming to steal women and children and take slaves. A quick and intimidating response was called for and that meant war canoes.

Now the war canoe is the racing canoe. The hull of the sleek racing canoe is fifty feet long. The hull and walls are adzed so thin that the canoe skims the water, much as a rowing shell does. Sometimes the dugout opening of the racing canoe is only as wide as the hips of the ones who will power it. Bill Holm— carver, scholar, professor—measured the old racing canoes at the Smithsonian. The thickness at the side may be only ¾ inch and the hull may be only 1½ inches—a small measure of cedar between those in the canoe and the ocean beneath them.

Modern-day racing at Lummi began in 1946. Warriors from World War I decided the returning warriors from World War II needed to be honored. So they founded Stommish, and the canoe races continued as Lummi warriors returned from the Korean War, the Vietnam War, the Gulf War, the Iraq War, and the War in Afghanistan.

Men race. Women race. Teenagers race. They race in the single, double, and six-person canoes. And they race in the long eleven-person canoe. Racers train for months or years. They say to get a place on the champion boat, paddlers have to train seven years.

Vi's friend Kenny Cooper, a big-voiced Lummi tribal leader, is the master of ceremonies. He stands up on a tower and speaks his big voice into a microphone so you can hear him all along the beach and beyond. People gather. They sit in the grandstand, stroll, buy fry bread or salmon, and play the bone game. They place bets on the canoe races, on the bone game, or on who has the most spirit power. At craft booths, weavers sell baskets, Cowichan sweaters and vests, or cedar bark headbands, visors, or rain hats. Tribal entrepreneurs sell T-shirts, sweatshirts, key chains, and baseball caps with Lummi logos or eagles, ravens, bears, salmon, or canoes on them.

The start gun sounds, and canoes surge across the water right in front of us. Muscle, adrenaline, and spirit power ride on the canoes. Carving skills are tested today, just as paddling skills

are. We watch race after race—the Indian Olympics. We breathe
in the excitement, the smell of fry bread, smoke, and salt water.

THE SUQUAMISH CANOE

Four years after the Paddle to Seattle comes the Paddle to Bella
Bella. 1993. Robby plans to make his own postage stamps for
tribal mail to be carried five hundred miles from Suquamish in
western Washington State up to Bella Bella in British Columbia.
Mail from one tribe to another, from one first nation to another,
will be stamped, postmarked, and delivered by canoe.

The Suquamish canoe captain and crew paddle across
from Indianola near Agate Passage on the Kitsap Peninsula to
Seattle, through the Ballard Locks, through the ship canal, under
the Fremont Bridge, under the Aurora Bridge, and across Lake
Union to our houseboat so Robby can take photos of the canoe
for the stamp design. We watch the canoe approach, watch it turn
for profile shots, watch it move through the water.

The captain brings the canoe alongside our deck. He invites
us to climb into the canoe. I sit on a small plank that runs
between the canoe walls and try to imagine sitting on that plank
for as many days as it would take to paddle to Bella Bella. One
young man entrusts me with his paddle. I place my left hand
over the top of the paddle and wrap my right hand around the
paddle's neck.

The captain calls out a command and I pull my paddle
through the water exactly as those in front of me pull theirs. In
the canoe I am flanked by red cedar, sit on red cedar, and pull
a red-cedar paddle. This wood is not fully red; it is copper red
or fox red or rust red or burnt red. I can smell the sweet sting of
thujaplicin, the potent oil red cedar releases when it is cut that
preserves the wood from rot.

We paddle past Ivar's Salmon House, where red-cedar dug-out canoes hang from the rafters. I don't look at people watching from the windows at Ivar's. I don't look at the people pointing at our canoe from Gas Works Park. I don't look south to downtown Seattle or the Space Needle. I follow the movement of the puller in front of me and remind myself to breathe. I imagine that I am at home in this canoe made of an ancient cedar tree. Back at our houseboat, I climb out—changed. We thank the captain in Lushootseed, offer juice and water to the crew. Then we watch the canoe take its leave, heading back past Gas Works Park toward the Ballard Locks, making the return trip across salt water to Indianola in Suquamish Country. Traveling around Lake Union in the red-cedar canoe is to them a training side trip; to us it is the whole journey and a blessing on our home.

Robby designs, prints, and perforates the canoe stamps. They depict the two dog-head canoes, one in profile with pullers wearing traditional rain hats, another canoe's prow in the foreground, dog head straining toward the first canoe. Rich blue ink on oyster-gray background. Copper-ink text. We go to Suquamish. Robby presents the stamps to the captain and receives a blanket of thanks. The canoe journey is on. Other tribes have traveled as far as Suquamish and are camped there before heading on to Bella Bella. The Suquamish Tribe feeds everyone salmon, venison, roasted potatoes, corn, and fruit pies. Speeches. Canoe songs. Paddle dances. Gifts. Blessings.

The next morning we go to Indianola. The captain of the Suquamish canoe takes the dry bag that contains mail from Suquamish to Bella Bella, franked by Robby's commemorative canoe stamps. The proclamation inside the envelope—written by the Suquamish and Duwamish people—declares the canoe post as valid mail.

The canoes launch. We watch the Suquamish canoe—*kaẃqs* (Raven)—slide into the water, watch until it disappears from view. I see each person pulling their paddle through water, and I imagine them pulling when dripping with sweat, shivering with chill, struggling against fatigue. The canoe will cross open water at the Strait of Juan de Fuca, travel up the Inside Passage, and again cross open water at Queen Charlotte Sound. How many paddle strokes will it take to travel five hundred miles?

THE CANOE JOURNEY CONTINUES

Since the 1989 Paddle to Seattle and the 1993 Paddle to Bella Bella, later canoe journeys have arrived at La Push, Puyallup, Ahousaht, Songhees, Pendleton, Squamish, Quinault, Tulalip, Chemainus, Elwha, Muckleshoot, Lummi, Cowichan, Suquamish, Makah, Swinomish, Squaxin, Nisqually, and other places along the Salish Sea. Emmett Oliver, the grand coordinator of the 1989 Paddle to Seattle when eleven canoes came ashore, lived to see the 2009 Canoe Journey at Suquamish when 110 canoes came ashore.

NEW CANOE

Vi Hilbert's aunt Susie Sampson Peter—a renowned cultural historian and healer at Swinomish—coined the phrase *to put information into a new canoe*. Her whole life, Aunt Susie had practiced telling all the stories she knew, even the complex epic stories that took hours to narrate. She spoke them aloud as she cooked, cleaned, and got ready for bed. All in Lushootseed. She worked to keep them fresh in her memory, for this was her job. When amateur archivist Leon Metcalf arrived at Aunt Susie's house at Swinomish with his reel-to-reel tape recorder, she looked at him and said in Lushootseed, "What took you so long to get here?"

Aunt Susie was ready to record everything she knew. She put the information on magnetic tape. Every story and every

teaching went into this new canoe, which she referred to as her
x̌əlayʔ. These tapes carried her words forward so that a decade or
two later, Vi Hilbert could transcribe and translate into English
each word her aunt Susie had spoken. Then Vi put those words
into books, onto cassette tapes, and later onto CDs, new canoes
that traveled out into the world after Aunt Susie was gone. Now,
Vi Hilbert too is gone. Yet all of this cultural treasure still travels, carried in the new canoe.

Now the new canoes are websites with archived recordings,
an online Lushootseed dictionary, YouTube videos, podcasts,
iPhone apps, #Lushootseed hashtags on Twitter, a daily weather
report, and video games based on stories from when animals
were people. No doubt all this will go into another new canoe,
one just now on the horizon, a canoe we don't yet know. But we
know it is coming, just as Aunt Susie knew that a new canoe was
coming, the one she had been waiting for all her life.

"In order for cultural information to travel, it had to have a
way to go forward," Vi said. "If you put this information in the
right way, then it can be metaphorically placed on a new canoe."
I think about Vi's words. I consider that the canoe itself carries
the culture in its form and material, in the way it is carved, and
in the people it carries between its walls. One canoe captain said,
"When we are traveling in our canoe, we are on a personal quest,
a pilgrimage to our ancestors' time." And at the same time these
canoes carry the culture forward to inform the future. The old
canoe is the new canoe.

gʷəqʷulc̓əʔ

Aunt Susie Sampson Peter

Vi Hilbert's aunt Susie Sampson Peter (book cover design by Robby Rudine)

Stamp used to carry mail by canoe during the canoe journey to Bella Bella (stamp by Robby Rudine)

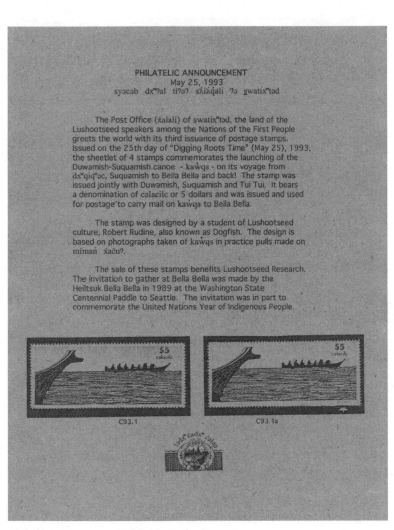

PHILATELIC ANNOUNCEMENT
May 25, 1993
syᵊcab dxʷʔal tiʔəʔ sʎiʎqali ʔə gʷatixʷtəd

The Post Office (ẋalali) of swatixʷtəd, the land of the Lushootseed speakers among the Nations of the First People greets the world with its third issuance of postage stamps. Issued on the 25th day of "Digging Roots Time" (May 25), 1993, the sheetlet of 4 stamps commemorates the launching of the Duwamish-Suquamish canoe - kaẇqs - on its voyage from dxʷqiqʷəc, Suquamish to Bella Bella and back! The stamp was issued jointly with Duwamish, Suquamish and Tui Tui. It bears a denomination of cəlacilc or 5 dollars and was issued and used for postage to carry mail on kaẇqs to Bella Bella.

The stamp was designed by a student of Lushootseed culture, Robert Rudine, also known as Dogfish. The design is based on photographs taken of kaẇqs in practice pulls made on mimaṅ ẋačuʔ.

The sale of these stamps benefits Lushootseed Research. The invitation to gather at Bella Bella was made by the Heiltsuk Bella Bella in 1989 at the Washington State Centennial Paddle to Seattle. The invitation was in part to commemorate the United Nations Year of Indigenous People.

$5 cəlacilc

$5 cəlacilc

C93.1

C93.1a

Philatelic announcement (by Robby Rudine)

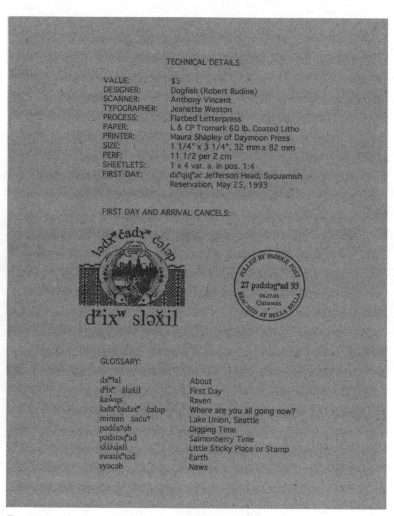

TECHNICAL DETAILS

VALUE:	$5
DESIGNER:	Dogfish (Robert Rudine)
SCANNER:	Anthony Vincent
TYPOGRAPHER:	Jeanette Weston
PROCESS:	Flatbed Letterpress
PAPER:	L & CP Tromark 60 lb. Coated Litho
PRINTER:	Maura Shapley of Daymoon Press
SIZE:	1 1/4" x 3 1/4", 32 mm x 82 mm
PERF:	11 1/2 per 2 cm
SHEETLETS:	1 x 4 var. a. in pos. 1:4
FIRST DAY:	dxʷqiqʷəc Jefferson Head, Suquamish Reservation, May 25, 1993

FIRST DAY AND ARRIVAL CANCELS:

ləxʷ čadxʷ čələp

dᶻixʷ sləx̌il

PULLED BY PADDLE POST

27 pədstəgʷad 93
06-27-93
Qatuwas

BEACHED AT BELLA BELLA

GLOSSARY:

dxʷʔal	About
dᶻixʷ sləx̌il	First Day
kaẁqs	Raven
lədxʷčadəxʷ čələp	Where are you all going now?
miman x̌aču?	Lake Union, Seattle
pədćaʔəb	Digging Time
pədstəqʷad	Salmonberry Time
sx̌ix̌qali	Little Sticky Place or Stamp
swatixʷtəd	Earth
syəcəb	News

Two stamp cancellations (by Peg Deam and Robby Rudine)

Robby Rudine and Vi Hilbert (photo by Janet Yoder)

Canoe on Baker Lake (photo courtesy Lushootseed Research)

THE BRAIN ROOM

Vi Hilbert ran a beauty shop called Vi's House of Curl in her Seattle home on Des Moines Way South until Lushootseed came calling. When Vi and Don built their house, they built the beauty shop off the kitchen with its own outer door. The house had a generous curved driveway with spaces for Vi's hair clients to park. Vi's granddaughter Jill La Pointe says, "I have fond memories of having my hair washed in that fancy shampoo bowl. It was so cool that my grandmother had one right in her home! And I remember as a little girl waiting patiently sometimes while Grandma had to 'bend hair' for a client before she could take me and my brother, Jay, on whatever the adventure of the day happened to be."

When Vi started her Lushootseed work, it was her general habit to spread that work out on her capacious table in the dining room, whose east window overlooked the activity at her bird feeder and the story places of the Duwamish Valley beyond. But she and Don (and anyone else who happened to be over) also ate at that table. At some point, Lushootseed needed more space, so Vi created space in her beauty shop. She told me that she still had a few favorite hair clients coming, so the room did double duty as Vi's life transitioned from hair bending to Lushootseed.

When Robby and I started coming to Vi's house, I remember the room having a hair salon sink, rolling salon stools, and a mirror. Then for Lushootseed purposes, it had a couple of tables, chairs, file cabinets, an old reel-to-reel tape recorder with stacks of tapes in labeled boxes, the boom box that she took to class to play cassette recordings, and a video camera. Shelves held books, videotapes, cassette tapes, and spiral notebooks full of Vi's handwritten transcriptions in Lushootseed. The IBM Selectric typewriter sat on a small rolling table.

The Selectric typewriter had a typeball—resembling a golf ball—that clicked into place. The ball rotated in every direction to present the correct letter to the page. A different ball for each font allowed the user to easily move between fonts. A company in Honolulu worked with linguists to make a special Salish version of their typeball using the International Phonetic Alphabet (IPA). That typeball allowed Vi to type Lushootseed using its particular orthography. Vi could remove the typeball with standard English letters and put in the Lushootseed one when needed. She used the Selectric typewriter for years and for much of her early material: vocabulary lists, grammar exercises, and dialog that we used in class. Though capable and relatively easy to use, the Selectric was still a typewriter. Vi couldn't go back and correct an error except with correction tape or Wite-Out fluid on paper. Or she'd have to type the page again. She had a copy machine and made copies of everything. But the Selectric typewriter was not a brain. Neither was the copier. In the early 1980s Vi's work was catching fire, and that work needed a brain.

Pam Cahn was one of Vi's Lushootseed students who became an expert in the computerized work for Lushootseed. Pam recalls that in 1982 Vi encouraged her to pick a Lushootseed project to work on, and she thought it would be valuable to update the 1976 dictionary by Thom Hess and Vi Hilbert.

Pam had no prior experience with computers but was aware that linguists at the University of Hawaii were using computers to compile dictionaries, including for Salish languages. Pam tells me that one of those linguists, Bob Hsu, had set up colleagues Larry and Terry Thompson with a Terak microcomputer for inputting data with user-designed IPA characters and printing on a Sanders printer with a custom Salish font. Pam explains that Terry Thompson arranged for the Terak sales rep to bring a computer to the Salish Conference in Portland in August 1982, where Terry gave a demonstration using the Terak to input a sample of her Thompson River Salish Dictionary: nɬekepmxcín data. The Terak rep told Pam there were several Teraks in use in Seattle, at Boeing and in a couple of departments at the University of Washington (UW). Pam secured permission to use one of these Teraks in the Academic Computing Center at UW during off-hours to begin entering Lushootseed data.

Enthusiasm for computerizing the Lushootseed dictionary grew, and Pam came up with a budget for a Terak microcomputer and a Santec dot-matrix printer with downloadable font capability for printing Salish characters, which Robby decided to fund. The computer and printer arrived in the fall of 1983. The purchase was arranged through the Upper Skagit Tribe to avoid sales tax. Pam drove up to Upper Skagit with Don Hilbert to pick up the equipment, which she then set up in her Seattle apartment. That allowed her to figure out how to use everything.

While Pam was at her day job, Jay Miller input *Haboo: Native American Stories from Puget Sound* into the Terak in her apartment, printing it out, camera-ready, for the University of Washington Press, on the Santec printer. Pam would then come home and work on the dictionary, the second shift for the Terak. After they finished entering all the new material, the computer and printer moved to Vi's house.

The gift from Robby to purchase the Terak triggered the creation of Lushootseed Research, the nonprofit organization Vi founded to preserve the language. Its incorporation papers were written and filed by Jack Fiander (Yakama), a former student of Vi's, who is now the tribal attorney for the Lushootseed-speaking Sauk-Suiattle Tribe. So in 1983, Vi suddenly had Lushootseed Research and a Terak computer to support her work. Anything was possible.

At Vi's house, the Terak moved into and quickly took over her beauty shop, which was soon renamed "the Brain Room." The Terak brought a true computer function to the Lushootseed work. Files in English and in Lushootseed could be saved, edited, reformatted if necessary, and printed. Vi knew the Terak increased the power of her work. To collaborate with her on projects, scholars came to the Brain Room, including Thom Hess, Pam Cahn, Jay Miller, Dawn Bates, Crisca Bierwert, Pam Amoss, Rob Hagiwara, and others.

The Terak was a brain, but it was not an easy brain to master, especially given that Vi was sixty-five years old when it arrived and had already struggled to recover from her first aneurism. The machine came with a detailed manual. Jay Miller distilled it into two pages of instructions to help Vi find her way into the world of the Terak:

Hi, I am YOUR Terak computer; do not be afraid.

The basic rule you need to follow is to know the screen is your friend. It will tell you what you can and cannot do. If the screen has the message that you want, press the letter for it. Otherwise, you have to tell the screen to find the command that you do want.

These commands are stored in boxes (the manual calls them "worlds"). The biggest box is F)ile. It helps you move things around.

Mostly you want the medium box called E)dit. That is where you enter and change around your texts. Q)uit moves you between boxes (worlds). It lets you I)nsert words and D)elete those you do not want. These are the primary commands. You can do other things in E, as the screen shows. They will be learned in time.

The smallest box is Lushootseed (because it is so special). Once you are inside it, other things cannot happen. So, to I or D or whatever, you have to come out of Lushootseed by pressing DC1, just like you pressed it to get into Lushootseed.

Now, let's go through the steps to enter texts.

Remove the covers off the machines you will use.

Turn on the disk drives.

Select the disk you will be using.

Put it in the lower drive (#4).

Close the latch by pushing it down.

Watch the screen.

If we are being good, we should indicate the date.

To do this, type F (big box) and watch for D)ate on the screen. Type D and put down today's date.

If it is a new month or year, put these down with - dashes between them, as day-month-year. Press Return key R.

Now we are ready to WORK.

Leave the File by typing Q for Q)uit, then E for E)dit.

Terak will ask the name of a file if you have already created one.

Otherwise, you need to hit R, the Return key. This will start you on a new file.

[page 2]

E will get you into the medium box, where you can I or D.

Make sure the cursor is in the spot where you want to begin. This saves time and hassles. Once you give it such a command, you can then move to the little box for Lushootseed.

(See manual pages 31–33 for I, 33–34 for D.)

Remember to save text with the ETX key every 4–5 lines.

After you do this, you have to get out of the little box so you can press I again. Then press DC1 and enter more text.

To REALLY SAVE your text, you must tell Terak to keep it for you.

You do this by pressing Q for Q)uit. The screen gives you four options, but only take the last one, W)rite. Press W.

Very carefully give it the name of the file.

Double-check this to be sure.

Then hit R for Return. If you have more text and time, then press R to R)eturn to where you left off.

Otherwise, hit E and E)xit.

You can now go on to other files or end that session (see manual page 22).

To end the session:

Unlatch #4 and carefully take out the disk. Keep it away from hard surfaces or bumps.

Put the disk back into its envelope— carefully. Close up the box. Turn off the drives. Cover up the machines.

No wonder Vi named it *sx̌alqəb* (Monster)! I confess that I never volunteered to do any work on the Terak. In 1983, I did not have a computer nor had I ever used one. Now as I read Jay's instructions for using the Terak, I feel overwhelmed by the complexity. It makes me grateful for my modern Apple computer, where I can toggle pretty expeditiously between a Lushootseed font and Times New Roman. It makes me admire Vi's tenacity in learning how to use this brain in order to further her Lushootseed work and place it in a new canoe.

I am not sure what happened to the Terak ultimately. But after four years, a new personal computer could do what the Terak did, as long as it had a Lushootseed font installed on it. Thus the Terak was replaced. Isn't that always the way? But in those four years, three significant Lushootseed books were written (or derived from files first written) on the Terak: *Lushootseed Dictionary* by Dawn Bates, Thom Hess, and Vi Hilbert, *Haboo: Native American Stories from Puget Sound* by Vi Hilbert, and *Lushootseed Texts: An Introduction to Puget Salish Narrative Aesthetics* edited by Crisca Bierwert. Sometimes these projects overlapped, giving the brainy Terak a good workout.

Beyond the Terak, the Brain Room is where other new canoes beached, the new technology or handy machines that helped Vi work on Lushootseed and also share it with the world. Over time, Vi went from reel-to-reel tapes to cassettes to CDs. In the Brain Room, she had a machine that duplicated cassette tapes and another that duplicated videotapes of every gathering she attended, every time she told stories or spoke. She kept stacks of those copied cassettes and videos in the Brain Room. When we went to Vi's house, she always gave us whatever she had just duplicated, a videotape or cassette tape, often with a Post-it with our names on it. She had a wide circle of recipients in Indian Country, in academia, and among her friends. She also mailed cassettes and videotapes to people who lived elsewhere. In a way, Vi was like Leon Metcalf, recording a message from one elder (or gathering) and giving it to the next elder (or person invited through her door). We were just lucky to be on the receiving end.

As work accumulated, the Brain Room also became Vi's archive. One day Vi and Don's house was broken into and a few things were stolen, including computers, but luckily not backup floppy disks. A computer is easily replaceable. Her basket collection was not touched. Nor was her archive. Vi said her thieves were too stupid to know what was valuable. But it was a wake-up call. Robby and I offered to store a copy of Vi's written archive at our office at *xʷaac ʔal ʔal* (Elevated House). Helpers duplicated everything and boxed it up. We stored it for years, until Vi and Don moved north to Bow, Washington, to live with her daughter, Lois. Vi asked us to transport her archive to her there because she was sharing information with tribal language programs and community colleges, while organizing the archive for the University of Washington. Special Collections at the University of Washington Suzzallo Library is the ultimate home for Vi's written work. You can visit the collection and get a sense of what came out of Vi's Brain Room.

In the end, when I think about that early Terak computer and the Brain Room at Vi Hilbert's house, I see that the brain was never the Terak. It was Vi's brain holding her memory of Lushootseed and the brains of all the scholars who worked with her that imbued the room with its braininess. The Terak was just one in a series of new canoes that carried the information further than it had gone before. And then another new canoe came along. Lately that same dictionary that was first input on the Terak has been put online. So you can access it right from your brainy smartphone anywhere you happen to be. You can also download the Lushootseed font to your laptop or phone quite easily. No need for a big boxy computer in a place called the Brain Room. The new canoe carries a Lushootseed brain that tucks right into your pocket.

Thom Hess working in front of the beauty shop mirror in the Brain Room
(photo courtesy Lushootseed Research)

Dawn Bates, Pam Cahn, Vi Hilbert, and Thom Hess in the Brain Room
(photo by Jay Miller)

HEALING HEART
SYMPHONY

It is *pədčaʔəb*, the time of digging cattail shoots—May. The people are going to Benaroya Hall in Seattle to hear the *Healing Heart Symphony*.

We gather in the outer hall, under the Chihuly glass chandelier, an opulent knot of pearlescent tentacles. The smell of Starbucks. Our breath comes fast, as if we had been chasing this day for a year, or longer. Everyone wears their finery: suits, flowing dresses, necklaces of amber and dentalium shells that resemble a long tooth, Pendleton wool vests and jackets, best flannel shirts, a boutonniere and a rain hat—both woven of cedar bark. We see people we know and love and too seldom see. We hear the call of a beloved name. Hug. Kiss. Camera click.

Is Vi here? We strain to see who gets off the elevators from the parking garage. Finally, it is Vi. Her vision is mostly gone; she holds niece Carmen's arm lightly, as if held aloft purely by anticipation. Vi, at eighty-eight, is petite but powerful. Her hair is short and still mostly dark. Her face radiates joy.

Her long-awaited day has arrived, the end of a sweet journey of expectation. Vi embraces one person after another, enfolding each of us in the drape of her soft red shawl.

"Aren't we lucky?" Vi beams. "We get to hear our symphony today." She doesn't say it is her symphony, though she commissioned it; nor does she say it is Bruce Ruddell's, though he composed it. It is ours. And the world's.

꜒꜖

First Movement: Prepare

Small shakers begin a heartbeat. Alone. Then violins join, ocean harp, and temple gong. Soprano sax sings the melody, plaintive like an Indian Shaker Church song. Violins rise and call like a voice. Breathy flute, like water caught in an eddy. Crescendo. Fortissimo. Then release, until only the bass and piano remain. Strike. Hold. Fade.

꜒꜖

Some gathering in Benaroya Hall have been Vi's students. Some are tribal people. Some were skeptical this symphony would come to pass. Some have been in her world a long time and know that when Vi wants something done, it gets done.

"I want to commission a symphony," Vi told composer Bruce Ruddell four years earlier. "I have a dream, a vision, in which two sacred songs need to inspire a symphonic work so that the power of those songs could start working again." She told him, "I want you to do this." Bruce had collaborated with the esteemed Haida artist Bill Reid to create an oratorio to tell the story of Mr. Reid's sculptural masterpiece *The Spirit of Haida Gwaii*. Bruce Ruddell was a composer who had already journeyed in Indian Country.

"I have no money," Vi told Bruce. Instead, she offered spirit songs: a Thunder Power song from Chief Seattle, entrusted to Vi by his descendants; and a Healing Song, bestowed upon her by her beloved cousin *pɔtius* (Isadore Tom) at the end of his life. "Use it when you need it, cousin," *pɔtius* had told her.

The events of September 11, 2001, made Vi sick at heart, and she knew the time had come. Vi placed these songs in the heart of the *Healing Heart Symphony*. She tendered them to Bruce Ruddell on cassette tapes. "They sat on my desk for some time while I tried to figure out how I would actually approach something like this," Bruce said. "So then one day, I took them in my backpack, along with a portable cassette machine. I went for a climb up Mount Erskine on Salt Spring Island. It's a beautiful climb up to the top, a great place to think or just be. I listened to them there at the top of this mountain. It was a beautiful day. I listened to them twice each. Then I put them aside, and I didn't listen to them again. At that time, the form of the piece came pretty quickly."

The songs cannot be used directly in the music. "Or," as Vi says, "the shit would hit the fan." A song is owned by a family. Others can hear the song, even be healed by the song. But the song belongs to the family. So Vi asked Bruce to compose a symphony inspired by these spirit songs, sacred songs, songs of the healing heart. "The Seattle Symphony is going to play it," Vi told Bruce, "and you will be paid properly." At the time, she had no agreement from the Seattle Symphony and, as she oft repeated, she had no money.

So other people drummed up the money for Vi's symphony, some from their own pockets. Friends of Vi's tucked money into her Pendleton wool handbag or slid money inside letters. Money came from the Seattle Foundation. Money came from the Tulalip

Tribe. Money came from the Tudor Foundation. When the word goes out, money travels in Indian Country. People shake hands and leave cash in someone's palm or slip folded bills into a pocket.

With this money, the symphony was composed. In summer 2002, we came to Vi's house in Seattle to hear those first two movements. We sat on sofas, armchairs, and dining chairs lined up in her living room, as if it were a small concert hall. Patricia Kim came as envoy of the Seattle Symphony. Bruce Ruddell stood in front of us. In a soft voice, he explained that the sounds we would hear were computer-generated and not as rich or distinct as an orchestra. His face flushed, as if he fought an urge to say more. He pushed the play button on Vi's boom box and sat down.

We listened. At times, the music rose to a continuous sound that I imagined would require much of the wind players. The score directs them to stagger breathing. Maybe money is like the air that blows from the musician's mouth into the mouthpiece and on down the grenadilla wood of the clarinet and oboe, or the silver metal of the flute, or through the rosy brass of the trumpet, trombone, and French horn. Shared, there is enough air, enough to keep the sound coming. And the strings bow steadily, changing direction with no break in sound. And it all keeps coming, as much as is needed, for as long as it is needed.

In *pədx̌ʷiwaac*, the time of robin song—April—2003, the symphony is completed. In 2005, Maestro Gerard Schwarz decides the Seattle Symphony Orchestra will perform it and he will conduct it. May 20, 2006, is the premiere of the *Healing Heart Symphony*.

⊓Γ

Second Movement: Thunder Spirit Power Song

The percussionist lifts Vi's father's drum into the air. The drum is named Captain and bears

a soaring eagle. The drummer beats a slow,
steady pulse that gathers the musicians one
by one. When all are present, the music rises
to voluminous sound, then calms, then builds
again. Wind arpeggios fly. Full orchestra plays
full chords that build to thick thunder, to rolling,
roiling, rising sound. Drop. Then rise again, to
the last three chords.

꘏꘏

We enter the lobby of Benaroya Hall and look out the wall of
windows at our glistening city: glass, steel, stone, salt water. We
gather in small groups that shift, then shift again, like slivers of
colored glass in a kaleidoscope.

Johnny Moses steps to the center of the lobby. Nearing forty,
Johnny is a small man with a huge voice. Johnny is Vi's nephew,
a brilliant storyteller, and a healer who carries the name Walking
Medicine Robe. He sometimes has his troubles: a couple of his
front teeth are now broken and his face shows faded bruises of
a recent beating that he says happened one night right here, in
front of Benaroya Hall. By asking him to address the crowd, "to
lay the carpet of spiritual understanding," Vi calls up the sublime
best of Johnny. He speaks of his auntie, of the symphony, of the
place where we are standing. "This land we are on is sacred. This
was a burial ground here." He points down through the floor.
"There's work that needs to be done." He sings Indian Shaker
Church songs, whose melodies rise like the most familiar Sunday
hymns. We all join voice.

꘏꘏

In Indian Country, Vi is known for commissioning work. She
had Alice Williams of Upper Skagit make her a cedar bark dress,

now on display at the Seattle Art Museum. She asked Ora Parent of Makah to string "Happy Bead" necklaces, named for the clicking of beads against olivella shells when the wearer moves. Vi asked Fran and Bill James of Lummi to weave her a thick wool blanket in traditional design. Vi commissions work to support the artists monetarily, to give recognition and praise, and to have the pleasure of giving these treasures to people she loves.

Vi receives her own assignments from her ancestors on the other side. Her beloved ancestors told her to heal through music. Music has a wider reach than words, especially words only spoken in western Washington's Puget Sound, and not even all of that. When asked why she commissioned a symphony, Vi joked, "Because I'm a bossy old Indian." In fact, she was doing the work given to her, and the work was healing her.

ᔑᔐ

Third Movement: Healing Song

The longhouse drum rolls. Soprano sax enters with the song, passes it on, then receives it again. The longhouse drum begins a steady beat, like a healing song. Gentle power. Phrases step down to close, bless, and heal.

ᔑᔐ

We enter the concert hall as if it is hallowed: a cathedral or a longhouse. Vi sits up front to listen to her spirit songs travel in a new canoe, deep inside a new work. The songs are now carried in the heart of the symphony. Or perhaps the songs carry the symphony. Vi's gift makes it possible. Why do some people give away what they value most, while others hoard it?

I remember Vi telling the story of Swallow, which comes from Tulalip elder Harriette Shelton Dover. Vi gave the story her own twist: Swallow was living there with all the other birds. The Changer came and saw that the birds had no homes. So he told them to build their homes. He showed them how to do it, how to make their nests. All did as directed, except for Swallow, who swished about, dressed up in her feather headband and bright beads, showing off her treasures. Then it was time for the Changer to come back and see all the birds' new homes. But Swallow didn't have a home; she didn't even know how to build one. So she took some mud and quickly made a house out of it. She built it big enough to hold all her treasures. She pulled her beads, jewels, and shiny bits inside her house. Then she mudded up the opening to protect her prizes. The next morning, the mud had hardened and Swallow couldn't get out. Poor Swallow— stuck inside there with all her treasures.

ᒣᒥ

Every time I visit Vi now at her apartment in La Conner, Washington, she gives me something. As I prepare to leave, she reaches for a paper she helped write for a museum catalog, or she goes to her curio cabinet to find a small basket, or to her entry closet to pull out a shawl. The second time she offers me a shawl, I resist. I take her hand and remind her she has already given me one, that I am honored to wear this beautiful reminder of her. She goes to the closet anyway. "Your mother might need this." She places the soft alpaca wool in my hands. So I accept and now my mother wears this shawl. Last time I visited Vi, we talked about the symphony, and then, as I gathered my tape recorder, she insisted on loaning me the music score.

You would think Vi's little apartment would be empty by now, with all the treasures she places in the hands of her visitors. But somehow treasures replenish. Visitors bring her gifts:

pints of fresh strawberries, a triple bouquet of daffodils, an Elvis
Presley CD. At gatherings throughout Indian Country, Vi rou-
tinely receives a blanket—or even once a nobility robe of mountain goat wool—to thank her for speaking, or just for being there.
Plus, Vi loves to buy things from Indian basket weavers, from
her daughter's alpaca ranch boutique, or from quilters who are
her neighbors at the La Conner Retirement Inn.

⊐⏸⊏

Fourth Movement: The Journey Forward

*Slow longhouse drumbeat. Vocalist speaks the
text in Lushootseed, sounds stretching out, a
recitation of credo. Falling lines in flute and
strings against rising lines in the piano. Wind
triplets. Soprano sax melody. Then faster, with a
gathering strength. Arpeggios build to thunder
power. Then a key change. Shift to healing. Lush
horns. Glockenspiel rings like Indian Shaker
altar bells. Continuous sound of prayer. Stagger
breathing. Share air. Share sound. Lushootseed
blessing: Ɂi yabid tiɁəɁ səliɁ. haydx̌ kʷi x̌aɁx̌aɁ.
gʷəkʷax̌acid (Honor the spirit. Know the sacred.
It will help you!).*

⊐⏸⊏

We sit in Benaroya Hall and let the music work on us. The four
movements make their journey around the four directions and
around the seasons; four is a sacred number in Vi Hilbert's part
of the Lushootseed world. For a year, we have carried this date,
the anticipation of this music, and Vi's intentions. We have carried them close to us. For a year, we have borne the fragility of

our elders; we have lost Vi's husband, Don, and then her son Ron. For a year, our gatherings have been in grief. For a year, we have waited. Now, the *Healing Heart* pierces my heart. I am grateful to be here, grateful Vi is still with us, grateful to receive this music, this gift.

⊓⌐

I consider gifts: Chief Seattle's gift of welcome to the arriving pioneers; the gift of Vi's cousin *pɔtius*, a renowned traditional healer, who got up from his own hospital bed because he was called to go do a healing on someone. I think about Vi's gift of this symphony. I think about giving, even when it seems little or nothing comes back. Or does it all come back?

"People that have passed on into other worlds are there to honor the gift," Vi says. "This symphony includes them, even though they are on the other side. I think this is the unspoken gift, that people on the other side are always with us to support the work."

⊓⌐

The last sound releases into air. The *Healing Heart Symphony* settles over us. I will its message into memory, direct it deep into my marrow to enrich my blood for the years to come when, if I am so lucky, I will receive assignments from the other side.

Larry Blain, Ellen Elizabeth Mae, and composer Bruce Ruddell
(photo courtesy Lushootseed Research)

Patricia Kim, Vi Hilbert, and Maestro Gerard Schwarz
(photo courtesy Lushootseed Research)

Vi Hilbert with Maestro Gerard Schwarz (photo courtesy Lushootseed Research)

Vi Hilbert in a blanket of cash with Carmen Shone in the lobby of Benaroya Hall (photo by Robby Rudine)

Vi Hilbert purchasing baskets from Isabell Ides (photo by Paul Eubanks)

RICH OLD INDIAN

The word for *money* in Lushootseed is *talə,* the Lushootseed pronunciation of the word *dollar.* Before the First People had money, Vi told me, a handmade blanket, a handwoven basket, a carved dugout canoe, or smoked salmon was prized currency. Even after the arrival of the *talə,* wealth in Indian Country was and is still measured by other means: by the quality of the naming you put on for your children, by the memorial for your departed, by the food you offer, by the gifts you give to each witness, and more than anything by the way you carry yourself. Your wealth may also be measured by the traditional name you carry, the stories you carry in your memory, the songs you have the right to sing, your spirit power, your rights and ability to fish and hunt, or your ability to weave baskets, build a plank house, smoke your salmon, or do traditional healing. Or your ability to recite the epic story of Star Child that takes hours to tell, a story that reveals how things came to be as they are now. If stories are wealth, then Vi was indeed rich. But she knew her ancestors were even richer.

Vi's father, Charlie Anderson, and his family were known as the head fishers of the Skagit River, as was the generation before them. That means they knew every bend, every eddy, every gravel bar where salmon laid their eggs, when and where the eagles would come to feed on spawned-out salmon, which family cared for and fished each part of the river, the health of the river, and the songs of the river. This knowledge was the family's wealth.

Having lots of relatives makes you rich. Though Vi was an only child, her folks claimed relations that stretched the bounds of kinship charts.

Vi was steadfast in her refusal to worry about money. She recalled, as a child, "When my folks needed cash, my mother would have me go to the door of a farmer to ask, *Do you want to buy any salmon?* I remember being rudely sent away. But when I'm selling books, I feel the same way. I'm selling fish." This may explain why Vi gave so many books away. When she had a project—publishing her books, commissioning a symphony, holding a naming or a memorial, she called on her spirit help and all of her volunteer helpers too. She repeatedly said, "Lushootseed takes care of itself." This means that the right people will get in the canoe and take up paddles, the money will come, and things will get done.

ᚱᚠᚱ

Vi helped people with money. She carried cash in an envelope in her Pendleton wool shoulder bag to every gathering. Then if she felt someone needed help, she would tuck money into someone's hands. She said the spirit guided her in this.

Consider the current trend of microloans made throughout the world to people, often women, to buy, say, a sewing machine that allows them to start a small business to provide for their family. Receiving the loan gives confidence, even status. Consider crowdfunding websites like Kickstarter or GoFundMe. This is money as help. When Vi helped others, the help was about the money but even more about the fact that Vi was signifying her belief in the recipient. A gift from Vi meant more than the amount of dollars she conveyed.

ᔐᒲ

Between living in a house that she and Don built, receiving whatever pensions and social security Vi had earned plus Don's pensions, including one from the Navy, Vi and Don were comfortable. They bought one piece, then another, of beach property at Point No Point near Hansville on the Kitsap Peninsula back when those properties were affordable. They had enough money that Vi could shop where she wanted to, take her friends and family out for a meal, and give money to those she wanted to help.

Certain tribal people accused Vi of getting rich off the culture, from teaching the language at the University of Washington or from her public speaking and storytelling. Vi did get paid for teaching and she sometimes got paid for public speaking. The money that came in helped fuel the next project she did. But sharing Lushootseed as far and wide as she could was her true reward.

Sometimes Vi needed big money to accomplish a particular goal, like founding Lushootseed Press to produce books of her elders' words that she had painstakingly transcribed in Lushootseed then translated into English so that those words could go out into the world. Vi refused to ask for money, but she would meet with someone who might be interested in her work. Or someone in her circle would apply for funding. If Vi wanted to make a film of elders telling stories, someone would write a grant. Somehow there would be enough money.

When you come from a childhood on a river where you can catch and smoke salmon, hunt duck, deer, and elk, travel down to the beach to dig clams, mussels, and oysters or harvest seaweed or goose barnacles, gather the tender shoots of fern, pick berries, dig potatoes or camas root, build your home out of cedar, warm yourself with a thick wool blanket, and travel to gather with people you love, you have no doubt about your wealth.

ЯГ

Vi had memorized many of the stories she learned from her ancestors and could tell them in both Lushootseed and English wherever she was invited to do so. She could speak to scholars or stand and speak in the longhouse. Vi brought Lushootseed out and gave it to the world, enriching all of us. Toward the end of her life Vi called herself a rich old Indian. Who could doubt that?

Vi Hilbert at a storytelling gathering at Upper Skagit (photo courtesy Lushootseed Research)

LUSHOOTSEED IS WRITTEN

For thousands of years, Lushootseed was an oral language. It had no written form. As I write these words, I consider how it would feel to speak a language that was not written, to have to memorize everything you needed to know—stories, even epic stories, longhouse speeches, a tribe's entire history.

As a child, Vi Hilbert learned Lushootseed as an oral language. Later she was amazed to see that Lushootseed could be written. She quickly learned how to write and read it.

Lushootseed is written using an orthography based on the International Phonetic Alphabet (IPA). The IPA is a powerful alphabet that can describe every sound made by any language on earth. Lushootseed does not use all the sounds in the world, but it does use some doozies like the glottalized barred lambda—an explosive click/crunch that shows up more often than we new learners might wish. So Lushootseed orthography uses forty-six characters of the IPA to express the sounds of the language.

When you first see Lushootseed written, it looks funny, uses symbols you don't recognize, and seems daunting to learn. But if you have ever taken a linguistics class and learned the IPA, then you already know the Lushootseed orthography. If you haven't, you can still learn to read and write Lushootseed in a short time. And you can apply that knowledge to any language expressed by the IPA. The "I" in IPA stands for "International," and the orthography truly is international. It is used by linguists and sometimes language learners and even opera singers. The IPA is not the only notation system out there, but it is the most universal. A linguist in Buenos Aires or Tokyo or Cairo will know how to pronounce Lushootseed words written with the IPA.

Over the years, Vi gave Lushootseed names and words for use in public projects. Today you can see Lushootseed written all over Seattle and Puget Sound. You can read Lushootseed in the concrete walkway at Alki Beach and in the sidewalk along Westlake near Lake Union Park. Vi gave Lushootseed terms for signs naming the plants that grow at the Olympic Sculpture Park and the Vi Hilbert Ethnobotanical Garden at Seattle University. She named the Butterfly House at the Woodland Park Zoo. Vi and her son Ron gave the Lushootseed text that is on display in the lobby of the Allen Library at the University of Washington (UW). It tells us that Raven brings light to this house of stories. Vi also named the UW longhouse wəɬəbalʔtxʷ, or Intellectual House. Recently, UW gave the name sluʔwił (Little Canoe Channel) to a campus road that runs alongside wəɬəbalʔtxʷ. There are plans to do more to recognize Native place names at UW.

In 2020, the Port of Seattle invited the public to nominate park names for parks along the Duwamish River. Many of the nominations were in Lushootseed, and so four parks on the Duwamish received their Lushootseed names. tuʔəlaltxʷ (Herring's House), sbəqʷaʔ (Great Blue Heron), həʔapus (Small Stream Draining Across a Flat on the West Side of the Duwamish River), and taɬtaɬucid (Where There Is Something Overhead or Across the Path).

The Tulalip Resort Casino displays beautiful art that features Lushootseed. The resort sometimes advertises its impressive hotel, spa, restaurants, shows, and casino in *The Seattle Times* and in regional magazines using written Lushootseed. Tacoma is working with the Puyallup Tribe to add Lushootseed to street signs. Organizations are asking for Lushootseed in land acknowledgments. At this point, it's not possible to keep up with all of the places that Lushootseed is appearing.

When I asked Vi how her folks felt about Lushootseed being written, she said, "They were so proud that I could pick up a piece of paper and read something that was in the language. That was something they marveled at." Vi told me all the elders wanted to see how it looked.

What happens when a previously oral language becomes a written language? Does it gain status? Permanence? Do its speakers then feel relieved that the language can be written, that they are no longer charged with holding everything in memory?

Vi was driven to publish books, produce recordings, and preserve everything she could. She wanted the work to be available to the future, to people not yet born. Lushootseed is expressed today in a large part because of Vi's devotion to speaking it, to teaching others to speak it, and to helping it take its place in the world as a written language.

We are comforted to think we have everything under the pads of our fingers, safely printed on paper, published in books, or stored in the cloud. But we must also keep Lushootseed—in whatever way we can—written in our hearts.

Vi Hilbert beside a Lushootseed art installation by Edgar Heap of Birds and a statue of Chief Seattle (photo courtesy Lushootseed Research)

LADY LOUSE
LIVED THERE

ʔəsɫaɫil kʷsi bəsč̓ad
ʔəsɫaɫil kʷsi bəsč̓ad ʔal te hikʷ ʔalʔal.
daỷuyʔ.
xʷiʔ kʷi gʷəsyayaʔs.
huy kʷədadəxʷ.
gʷəl ʔuʔiq̓ʷidəxʷ tiʔəʔ hikʷ ʔalʔal.
qa sč̓iq̓ʷil.
x̌ʷuləxʷ uʔudəgʷiɉələxʷ ʔal ti ʔalʔal.
huy x̌ʷiləxʷ.
šəbšub bəsč̓ad.
diɫ shuys.

Lady Louse Lived There
Lady Louse lived there in that great big house!
All alone.
She had no friends or relatives.

Then she took it.
And she swept it.
That great big house.
There was lots of dirt!
When she got to the very middle of the house,
she got lost!
That was the end of Lady Louse.
That's all.

Lady Louse (drawing by Kenneth Greg Watson)

What an odd little story. Why did Lady Louse live in a great big house all alone? Why didn't she have any friends or relatives? Why did she take it and sweep it? Why was her house so dirty? Why did she get lost? Why was she a louse to begin with? And why does Vi tell this story everywhere she speaks?

We wonder all these things when we meet Lady Louse for the first time, maybe even the second, third, and fourth times. But eventually Lady Louse settles in, as lice are wont to do, and we begin to think we might know who she is and why she lived there.

Elizabeth Krise told the story of Lady Louse to linguist Thomas Hess in 1962. She told the story in her native language, Lushootseed, and he recorded it for his research. Later he shared the story with Vi and asked her to transcribe and translate it. Vi did that, and then she adopted the story of Lady Louse.

When Vi taught at the University of Washington, she used this concise story to help students learn the Lushootseed language and peek through a knothole into her culture. She asked each student to create an original Lady Louse story and tell it to the class. She asked her friends and relatives to do the same. Vi views the stories Lady Louse inspired as a kind of Lushootseed Rorschach test, each representing one listener's take on poor Lady Louse's demise. This petite insect being shines a pinpoint light that allows us to see the Lady Louse hidden inside us. We might be able to laugh at what we see. Or cry. Or simply see her. This is the gift Lady Louse offers.

Cover of Lady Louse Lived There
(designed by Brad Burns)

THE BONE GAME

You go into the world of the bone game. It is 1978. The game is in Vi Hilbert's Lushootseed class in Denny Hall at the University of Washington. It is your first quarter of Lushootseed. You struggle with the complex clicks and throat-clearing sounds required by the rich speech of the First People, struggle with syntax, struggle with identifying the root of each word and the particles attached to it. Everything is new and hard, and you don't know how lucky you are to even be in this classroom. On this day, Vi brings in bones and tally sticks for a bone game. You believe the bone game is just a game, a gamble. You think you win by luck.

⊓⌐

Robby and I drive north from Seattle to the Tulalip Casino. Tulalip was and is—partly thanks to elders Vi Hilbert, Harriette Shelton Dover, Marya Moses, and others—a Lushootseed-speaking tribe. One of Vi's early students, Toby C. S. Langen, became a linguist with the Lushootseed Language Program at Tulalip. As we travel, I consider Vi's generosity, her willingness to teach her language to anyone who enrolled in her class, to share recordings of her ancestors and elders, to share the songs and stories that teach us how to live in this place.

⊐∥⊏

Vi encouraged us to put our thoughts—admittedly simplified—into Lushootseed. And she encouraged us to play the bone game to get a glimpse into the culture. I didn't know Vi well when I was first in her class. I didn't know until years later that she never played the bone game herself except in class. "I did it in the classroom because that was safe," Vi said. "My students and I had fun seeing who could outsmart one side or the other."

⊐∥⊏

Vi tells you about the bone game—called sləhal—how it was a way to settle a dispute peaceably, how it was a spiritual competition, a test.

Vi tells you how to play. Two teams line up to face each other, sitting on the ground or a bench. Team One selects a leader who has two pairs of bones—four bones total. The leader chooses two players, and each of these players holds a pair of bones, one bone in each hand. The female bone has a colored band—like a dress sash—painted around its middle. The male bone is unmarked. Team One sings its song accompanied by the beat of hand drums. During the song, the two players holding the bones hide their hands behind their backs or under a blanket and they move the bones around. Then they bring their hands into view, their grips covering the middle and therefore the gender of each bone. The song ends. Team One's leader will motion to the leader of Team Two that it is time to guess the location of the male bone. If the opposing leader guesses incorrectly, he gives up a tally stick. There are eleven

tally sticks in all. If the opposing leader's guess is correct, then
the bones are passed to his team for a round.

᠎ᔕᖀ

We arrive at Tulalip. Inside the hotel lobby, we see a carved
cedar pole with a figure on top, hands raised in welcome. A second carved cedar pole depicts Bear with a Tulalip woman and
a wolf/man. We are drawn to the third pole. It is a bone game
player who holds a bone inside each of his raised fists. The ends
of the bones are visible above and below the fists. The middles
are hidden, leaving us to guess which bone is male and which
is female. The bone game is a gambling game, and the Tulalips
are making the connection between this cedar carved figure of
an ancient bone game player and all the people gambling next
door in their casino.

᠎ᔕᖀ

Vi brings out a pair of bones—small, cylindrical bones—cut
from the foreleg of a deer. She passes the bones around. You feel
the smooth, much-handled surface of the bone in your palm, and
you can just feel the incised band of the female.

᠎ᔕᖀ

Some tribes own land in a great location, say near Seattle or
Tacoma, or right along Interstate 5 or Interstate 90. Those tribes
build casinos that bring in lots of people. Those tribes adver-
tise on billboards, in travel magazines, and on TV. They show
cool guys and gorgeous women in dazzling dresses and sparkly
jewels, ecstatic over their luck at roulette. Those tribes bring in
big names from the '70s and '80s: Diana Ross, Aaron Neville,
Gordon Lightfoot, Tower of Power, and Huey Lewis and the

News. The message: come to the casino, have a drink, eat dinner, see a show, then sit at a blackjack table and become a winner.

We are here in the daytime and people don't look like the TV ads. Most wear jeans or sweats. Some have a cigarette going. Many are middle-aged or older. But they are here testing their luck.

Vi shows you the eleven tally sticks. They are a foot and a half long and cylindrical with a point at the end—like extra-long pencils—to be stuck in the ground. Each bone game team starts with five tally sticks. The bigger eleventh stick—the king stick or kick stick—moves only at the end of the game.

Vi Hilbert's tribe, the Upper Skagit, decided to build a casino along I-5 north of Burlington. They hired Harrah's to open it. They asked for Vi's blessing. She gave her support but asked that each tribal employee take a weekly Lushootseed class at the reservation, which she would teach. The class started out with a good number but dwindled.

Vi divides your class into two teams—two tribes. You are with the tubšədə (the Yakama) because you grew up near the Yakima River in eastern Washington. The other team is the Skagit, Vi's tribe. You know as soon as you face each other that the Skagits will win because Vi is Skagit, because your classroom is in Lushootseed Country with all the power of home team advantage.

The two teams face each other. Your class is about one-third ʔaciłtalbixʷ (Indian) and two-thirds pastəd (white [literally

Boston*]). Captains of both teams are ʔaciɫtalbixʷ. Your captain is from Yakama and he chooses a woman on your team to hold one pair of bones and he holds the other pair. The captain begins singing. A teammate beats a drum. The bone holders pull their hands behind their backs and mix the bones, as if playing hide the thimble. They each hold a bone in each hand. Four hands. Four bones. Though they are your teammates, you do not know which two fists hold male bones and which two hold female bones. The bone holders bring their fists around in front of their bodies. They move their fists in time to the song, move their fists in arcs in front of their bodies and over their heads. It looks like their fists are dancing. You see that some of your classmates have played the bone game before. All you can do is sing.*

Vi talks about how tribes have put casino money into language programs, teacher training, classes for young children, computer software, and bringing the language out. Vi agrees that these things are good. But she tells me that she cautions the tribes with big casinos not to make themselves big, *ʔiʔabcut*, but instead to make themselves high-class and respected *siʔab*. She expresses great pride when she observes them doing this.

The Yakama song ends and the Skagits must guess. They discuss among themselves and then their guesser points to the hand he believes holds an unmarked bone. He is correct. Your team hands over its first of five tally sticks. The Skagit captain takes the stick and digs it into the ground, but there is no ground because you are in a classroom.

June 2008: I visit Vi at her apartment in La Conner. She is nearly ninety and fragile. Vi says, "The bone game was a man's game. My dad played; my mother never did. We watched but we didn't play." Vi tells me about her father. "His power was stronger than anybody else's. He could spiritually see into the hands of his opponent and know where the correct hand was that would give him the winning bet. The competition was very, very serious. I was told that it was a test of mentality but also a test of spirit. Your spirit helped you if you were bone gaming. You had to be careful not to offend the spirit."

∏∏∏

In your Lushootseed class, the Skagits launch their song and you watch the four hands that hold bones. Your bone game goes on less than an hour because you are in class and the bell will ring. The Skagits win and the Yakama lose. You eat Waverly Wafers spread with cream cheese full of smoked salmon afterward. You thank Vi for the bone game. Then you go to your next class.

∏∏∏

June 2008: Vi talks about songs sung during a bone game. "They had songs that went with the gaming. You'd hear the tempo change every now and then. A new song would be started. Everybody would be enthusiastically chiming in." I ask Vi if bone game songs are only sung at the bone game. "I have heard songs that have been a part of the Indian Shaker religion and part of the longhouse," Vi says. "I have seen how they've been able to change those just a tiny bit. Elders have shown me how that can be done. The tempo will change just a little bit. You recognize it as a longhouse song, but it is now a gambling song."

A family owns the song it sings. "You don't sing somebody else's song," Vi says. "Because the songs are recognized.

Because songs are known. People are chosen for their voices and their strength. If they know that this person has a good song that can help a winning team, then that person with a strong voice would be invited to sit on that team. You hear the voice initiate a new song when a side is losing. If you pay attention, you can hear the strong song come to pick it up. And the betting gets bigger."

⌐Ir⌐

Years after Lushootseed class, when you are friends with Vi, you go with her to the Stommish grounds for the canoe races at Lummi. You watch strong paddlers pull the eleven-man cedar racing canoes through salt water. Then you turn around and there is a bone game behind you. You approach and it feels as if the game has gone on for days, and maybe it has. You see a woman wearing a cedar bark visor and you see her eyes follow the other team's hands as if those hands are puppets that she controls.

⌐Ir⌐

In the casino, Robby and I leave the Tulalip poles. We walk past large spindle whorls and under metal salmon that hang from the ceiling to reflect light from the clerestory. We study the cedar bark mats, rain capes, baskets, and dolls. Then we see a set of tally sticks for the bone game.

The resort connects to the casino. An inset carpet delineates a path to follow, blue swirling patterns like a fast river with eddies. We walk the river of carpet. The whiff of cigarette smoke tells us we have arrived in the casino proper. Pendent lights curve overhead. Slot machines give off electronic burbles. The machines come in groups: Wild Wolf, Timber Wolf, and Wolf Run; Wild Panda, Lotus Flower, and Triple Fortune Dragon; Pyramid Plunder, Cleopatra, Sphinx, and Pharaoh's Fortune.

I sit down at a slot machine called Secrets of Stonehenge and insert a five-dollar bill. The slot machine is all-electronic—no lever to pull. Squares show owls, falcons, horses, swords, and goblets. My scoreboard displays the points my five dollars purchased. I press the button to bet one hundred points. The squares flash and then settle. My owl squares blink to show I have won points; I have also lost points. The tally is kept in two columns. I press the button again. I win and lose. I press again. Overall I am down a bit, but don't feel like I am losing because I almost always win some points. I am surprised at how long the game lasts. Casinos have state-of-the-art air-handling systems, but there is always smoke and more smoke as the day progresses. I press the "Bet It All" button, thinking that will end the game. Again, I win and lose. I keep pressing that button and on the fourth time, I win lots of points, more points than I started the game with. So I press the "Cash Out" button and a ticket for $6.50 slides out of a slot.

I take my receipt to a cashier's window. A young woman hands me a five, a one, and a fifty-cent piece. The coin feels good in my palm, like luck.

ᓚᖰ

At Lummi with Vi, the song pounds with a furious beat, faster than horses. The song races itself and pushes the game. Someone taunts the guesser. "Are you blind?" they shout, as if everyone else can see right through the hands, see inside the fists, see what they hold. The song is loud, money moves in side bets, the crowd deepens, tension builds. You feel dizzy and you can't keep your eyes on everything. You know there is big money riding on those bones. The song ends. The guesser gestures his guesses. Hands open. Shouts. Laughter. Release. A tally stick moves. Money moves. Then another round begins. You see this is the real thing, not the game you played in class.

⊐∥⊏

When the First People of the Pacific Northwest gather during summer, a bone game will often start up. The players do not wonder whether this is their lucky day or if these smoothed pieces of deer bone are their lucky bones. Players face opposing players. They call on their power, their help, their guides, call on their winter of spirit dancing in the longhouse, their fasting, and their praying. They call on all that they carry—a traditional name, the stories they know, teachings from their elders, messages from ancestors they know only through the veil. They call on their *x̌əčadad*—the ability to use mental powers to effect some change in the physical world. They call on all this as they take up the bone game.

⊐∥⊏

Another round ends at Lummi. You see money move from pockets onto a blanket, into a basket, a woolen pouch, or other pockets. You try to follow but it feels like you are on the floor of the stock exchange watching buys and sells that will never catch up to the force of the market.

⊐∥⊏

I consider luck and I consider spirit power. I know Vi had spirit power. Some said she had mountain goat power, to help her walk a perilous high path while keeping balance. Was it just my good luck to walk through the door of Vi's classroom in the fall of 1978, my good luck that she chose Robby and me to be part of her closer circle, that she invited us to go with her to the longhouse, work on her Lushootseed projects, and be in some way part of her world?

ᔑᔐ

In 1987, a farmworker installing an irrigation pipe found a set of mastodon bones—some of them shaped and marked like unusually large bone game bones—in an apple orchard in East Wenatchee, Washington. The bones are now at the Burke Museum and the Washington State History Museum in Tacoma, where the largest is on display. Tests show those bones are nearly fourteen thousand years old. Are they bone game bones? Large ones meant for special use? Archaeologists are not sure, though some say it seems reasonable. There are tribal leaders who believe the bones go back to an ancient bone game.

Vi Hilbert's bone game set (photo by Jay Miller)

Historic photo of bone game team at Lummi (photo by Eugene H. Field, courtesy University of Washington Libraries)

BECOMING AN ELDER

Vi Hilbert was sixty when I met her. She did not call herself an elder.

Years later I asked Vi about becoming an elder. She said, "Elder doesn't mean old. An elder looks at responsibility to the culture they come from and takes on the responsibility for working to keep that culture alive. They become an elder at any age. Sometimes it might be teenage, or well before old age. Sometimes it's after they have matured. There is no given age at which a person becomes an elder. I always felt it was going to be up to my mother and my dad to keep everything alive. It was never up to me. But after they died, people turned to me to talk. I didn't feel qualified to talk. I don't know anything. My parents were the ones who knew everything. I can't ever do that the way my parents did. I asked my cousin Dewey Mitchell, *When you talk, it seems so easy. You just talk. Everything that comes out of your mouth is so wise and meaningful. How do you do that?* His response to me was *It gets easier every time you have to talk.*"

꩜

Vi called to tell me that Ivy Guss had died. Ivy would no longer sit next to the altar, as is an elder's right, to be close to the cross and the handbells that will be rung along with the Indian Shaker Church songs at Vi's gatherings at the Medicine House.

At the funeral, each speaker thanked everyone who came to honor Ivy's life. Each speaker acknowledged Vi. "She is our elder now," they said. "We must treasure her." My throat tightened as everyone turned to Vi. I wonder how she felt seeing herself lifted to the top. Ivy Guss was in her nineties when she passed away. Vi was eighty-six, though when speaking she tended to add to her years. "I'm almost a hundred," she told a crowd, making us think she could hardly become more of an elder than she was just then.

꩜

Elders get lots of perks in Indian Country. An elder is picked up at home and driven to a gathering, seated up front in the longhouse on a chair draped with blankets. An elder takes a place of honor at a memorial or burning, or at a First Salmon Ceremony. An elder is served the first plate of food. An elder is wrapped in a blanket, asked to speak at a naming. An elder is listened to, especially if that elder speaks Lushootseed. An elder is a resource. An elder is sought out and sought after. An elder will lend status to your gathering.

It is good to be an elder, better to be an elder who remembers the old words, the stories, and the old ways, an elder who carries the culture and delivers it to the next generation. Best to be an elder who still has work to do. Over time, Vi became one of the most sought-after elders in Lushootseed Country.

꩜

November 2008: Seattle Art Museum hosted a show called *S'abadeb (The Gifts)*. Vi gave the show its name. I stood by her wheelchair at the show's dedication. I didn't know it was my last visit with Vi. Did she know? Is that something else that comes with being an elder, knowing when your time is winding down, knowing when to reach out and hold someone's hand, when to speak from the heart, when to look forward to the spirit world, when to hear your folks calling to you, when to begin releasing your hold on the gifts you have received and the gifts you have carried, when to pass those gifts to your chosen ones, the ones who will carry those gifts forward, ones you hope will one day become elders?

Vi Hilbert surrounded by cultural treasures (photo courtesy Lushootseed Research)

BURNING AT NOOKSACK

"They're going to burn my folks' house up at Nooksack." Vi's voice is soft over the phone. "Because there was already a fire there, and now it has to be demolished."

I look out my window. Winter rain falls into Seattle's Lake Union, and I can't imagine anything burning. "They can't repair it?"

"No. They're going to burn it for my folks. To send it to them in the spirit world. The date is set." Her voice sounds both bleak and sure. I know there is more to the story. "Will you and Robby be my drivers?"

"Of course, *tsi siʔab*," I answer right away, speaking for my husband too. Vi has invited us to travel with her over the years—to the Tulalip Longhouse during the winter spirit dance, to canoe races at Lummi, to observe a bone game with cash bets and spirit power riding on it, to witness a young person receive his traditional name, and to visit the story places. Vi blessed our marriage with a cedar bark fishing basket that sits on our highest shelf. Now, when she asks if we will be her drivers, there is only one answer.

⊓⌐

The day comes dark, barely day at all. Low clouds travel over salt water and cloak flat Skagit land. We drive north from Seattle to Vi's house in Bow, Washington.

"I've been awake since three o'clock this morning," Vi says. Her face doesn't look tired, just thin. These days she is smaller in person than in my memory, and I must bend to embrace her.

"Will you be warm enough, *tsi si?ab*?" I ask. Vi shows me her layers against the chill: cotton turtleneck, cashmere sweater, quilted jacket, silk long johns, heavy pants, and leather loafers. Then there is her thick shawl.

We drive north on the freeway to Bellingham, then east on the Mount Baker Highway, then north on Everson Goshen Road. After that Vi tells us where to turn. "I'm blind, you know," she reminds us. We laugh. Often she still knows the way, but on this day we overshoot our destination and end up in the town of Lynden. We drive through town on empty Sunday streets. I call Vi's grandson, Jay, and his wife, Bedelia, from my cell phone. Bedelia gives us directions. We turn around and head for Everson. Vi is not daunted by our trip to Lynden. It's all an adventure. Anyway, we started out twice as early as we needed. I think Vi hopes for detours. More time in the car to visit.

It's still early when we arrive at the home that Vi's father built for her mother in 1935. It is a compact wooden house, with overlapped cedar siding painted white, which stands out against the winter gray and the rain-laden cedar trees. The house is smaller than I remember, smaller than in Vi's words. "My mother welcomed visitors to her home. Sometimes they stayed for days, and that made my mother happy. This was her palace."

We park across the road in front of a plastic red-nosed Rudolph pulling Santa's sleigh across a neighbor's yard. Vi hasn't witnessed the damage to the house; from the car, it looks whole. She hesitates, then climbs out. We walk around to see where the recent fire burned. We peer in at blackened walls. Outside, charred siding glistens in the rain.

Vi is quiet, controlled. Finally she speaks. "This house was my mom's reward. After years of moving up and down the Skagit River, to Concrete, Birdsview, and little places between Lyman and Marblemount. Those places don't have names in English. We moved where my dad could get work. Sometimes he fished, or picked fruit; sometimes he cut trees and floated logs down the river." I've seen photos of Skagit men standing in shovel-nose canoes. They use pike poles to guide logs on the river, like cowboys herding cattle along the trail. "We were always moving. Sometimes living in a garage or a chicken house. Finally he built her this house."

We huddle under a cedar tree where there is a little less rain. The world is saturated with moisture, the house a wet ghost.

Jay and Bedelia arrive. Both are thin and wear long hair. Hugs all around. The couple raised their children in this house, then they built a new house farther back on the land and rented this one out. But I remember bringing Vi to this home a dozen years ago on a summer afternoon. We were on our way north to a Salish Conference up in Kamloops, British Columbia. Then the place smelled of buttery shortbread, ginger tea, Play-Doh, and Mr. Bubble. Now it smells of char.

"The tenants weren't hurt in the fire," Bedelia says of the now-gone neighbors. "But their dog and cat were killed." We groan. The loss of animals hangs close, making the fire somehow intimate.

Marilyn Wandrey of Suquamish joins us. Her father, Lawrence Webster, was a dear friend of Vi's. Marilyn has taken

Vi's Lushootseed class and sought Vi's guidance as she made her way into tribal leadership at Suquamish.

Bedelia sets up a lawn chair and spreads a blanket across its seat. Vi sits. We wrap her in a shawl and, over that, a diamond-patterned Pendleton blanket with buffalo across it. Her alpaca wool hat sits atop her head. I hold an umbrella over her as if she were royalty, which—in Indian Country—she is.

A caravan of cars and trucks pulls up. "There's our ritualist," Vi says. Dorothy Charles and her family hop out. Less than five feet tall, Dorothy is the shortest, the oldest, and clearly the one in charge. She is broad and solid. Wiry hair. She wears a woven cedar band on her forehead and a light wash of red paint across her cheeks. I look around and see that her family wears the same face paint. Ready for spirit work.

Dorothy greets Vi. They talk about Vi's parents. Dorothy lives just down the road and knew them. "All my kids live right here," Dorothy tells Vi. "Within a half-mile of me." She grins. "Or they live with me."

"You are a rich woman, then." Vi opens her arm to include Dorothy's crew. "All this family around you."

Jay tells Dorothy that the fire captain suggested they do the ritual but not burn the house. "The fire department wants to burn it later as training."

"We need to burn the house today for Vi's folks," Dorothy says. Jay nods. This is what he expected, what we all expected.

Everyone looks to Dorothy. She signals to the men in her family, who are dressed for outdoor work, in blue jeans, flannel shirts, sweatshirts, jackets, knit hats, or baseball caps, men who look capable of doing anything Dorothy might ask. They carry kindling and paper from their trucks. They go to each corner of the house. They lean scrap wood against each corner and tuck in newspaper wads. I can't tell if they have been assigned to their corners or are simply used to working together. Young boys help.

The women gather around Dorothy. Girls, too. Full faces and strong bodies in warm jackets. They pull drums out of bags. And drumsticks, beating ends padded with deerskin. They pound to warm up, skin thudding against skin, the sound swallowed by rain. This doesn't slow them down. If anything, it sparks them. Dorothy sings. Her voice rises like a strong prayer, and I strain to hear if it is in Lushootseed or a more northern language. The song is more vowels than consonants and I can't be sure. Her family joins in. We join too.

After one full round of the song, Dorothy signals the men to move from the corner each has prepared to the next corner. Drums pound. We sing again, and the men move again. Signal. Drums. Song. The men arrive at the fourth corner, nearly completing a journey around this house. We sing once more, and the men return home, each to his corner. We have sung them around the house, around the four directions, the seasons, the four times a story must be told or a song sung. Drums pound to a finish.

The four fires light. Paper. Then sticks. The flames are wispy, flimsy. They require tending. I stand behind Vi with my hands on her shoulders. I feel her shudder as the fire catches, and then she nods her head. Reluctant fire clings to the damp house exterior. Still, fire finds a means to burn, to draw on the seasoned wood just inside the house. Fire finds fuel.

Dorothy stands with her women: daughters, daughters-in-law, nieces. They watch their men feed wood into the corner fires. Dorothy directs. More kindling over there. She points at a corner that gets no help from the wind.

I crouch beside Vi in her chair, take a sideways look. Her face appears tiny under her hat. Her eyes peer through her glasses that once fit but now seem too large. The set of her jaw shows determination. She is here to witness this work.

Walls catch. White paint spits as it heats. Its quick chemistry fuels the fire. The western corners take. Fire scales the walls and curls through windows, then travels across the lapped cedar planks that side the house.

The sky remains dark. Air stays cold, so that the fire's heat begins to stand out. I see smoke rising off the house. The walls come alive. They groan and creak. Paint sizzles. Pipes crack. My nose twitches with the smoky mix of seared enamel, blistered varnish, and burnt wood.

The women begin to talk. The men tend their corners. Sometimes they poke at the burning wood with a pike pole, nudging it inside the house as if urging in a hesitant visitor. The flames edge toward each other like lovers who sense each other's heat.

Vi watches the flames, the house, maybe her ghosts.

"This house was my father's love gift to my mother," she says. "He built it for her. To make her happy."

The fires crackle as they reach for each other. I peer through the flames and see Vi's father sawing cedar, hear him pounding wood to wood, framing up this palace for Vi's mom. I strain to hear his song. He did a lot of singing. Vi shared tape recordings of his songs for fishing, for working, for healing. In my mind he sings a love song as he hammers together this house of cedar. His voice rises, and then the fire takes over the song. The fire becomes a song. A gift.

Vi's mother will receive this house again; Vi's father will receive her happiness again. The four fires meet inside the house. Flames draw together in electrical arcs that charge the house back to life.

A green pickup truck pulls up. A lanky man gets out and ambles over to us. He nods at Vi then tells Robby he is the fire marshal. Robby tells him it's a ritual burning. The man nods. Clearly, he already knows this. Robby sends him over to talk with Jay. The two of them walk together around the house. When they come back around to our side, they shake hands. I hear the man say he will tell the dispatchers to ignore any 911 calls. He climbs in his truck and drives off.

We turn back to the fire. Entire walls burn, large flames that reach up toward the roof. One wall bulges outward. The men buttress it in place with a long two-by-four. Though we are sitting fifteen feet from the house, I feel its increasing heat. The fire seems to mix up the wind, sending black smoke our way. Now I see that the whole house will burn. There is no stopping the flames. All of it will burn.

The fire flares high, and Dorothy approaches us. She speaks with a calm you do not expect from a lady burning down a house. "Maybe you should move your elder back." She points us to a cluster of trees farther from the flame, heat, and smoke. We unwrap Vi from her blanket and shawl. It is like peeling a thick breading from a prawn, which turns out to be surprisingly small, for all its flavor. Vi takes my arm and we journey to our new camp. Robby seeks level ground for her chair. I feel Vi shiver and wonder if she wanted to be close to the fire. Or is she shivering because we are so close to the spirit world? I bundle her back into layers. Her eyes return to the house of flames.

Dorothy addresses me as Vi's family. Should I tell her I am not? Vi calls us her Lushootseed family. Sometimes she addresses me as her adopted daughter. I remind myself that Vi adopts a lot of people, as if we are strays, foundlings, or lost beings. It's a big family that Vi gathers in her basket and carries into her world. Still, my skin warms when Vi says *daughter*, and my pulse strengthens. I feel this adoption in my breath, which comes out like a deep sigh that drops low and settles.

⊓⌐

Smoke follows itself in and out of openings in the house walls like children playing crack the whip. The fire strengthens. Flames rise up the four walls, licking around eaves and onto the roof. The burn continues until the shape of the house is outlined by flames, an architecture lit into vibrant design, radiant against the gray damp of winter.

The cedar tree nearest the house catches fire; it flares for a second and then its wetness quenches the flame. Rain drips from branch to branch, and water weighs down boughs. It is the tree we were first sitting under. We watch the house burn from our new vantage, and Vi's memories warm. "My folks always kept their door open, so that anyone could come to this house. People in Indian Country knew that." The fire now burns through the kitchen. "My mom always had bread baking and a big pot of soup on the stove, so she could toss in smoked salmon to feed more folks." I am sure I smell this food.

We witness the work. Flames find their way through the roof. A roof of fire. The shape of the house is as large as it will get, in blazing illumination. Flames surge from its peak, toward the wet sky. I will the image to stay in my memory.

The roof crashes to the floor. Orange flames roar, and heat hits our faces. Nothing contains the fire. It burns out of the box, and it burns the box. A wall wobbles and threatens to fall. The helpers use a pike pole to push it into the interior. What had been standing now lies down, still burning. After a time, the second wall falls, pushed by shovels with blade metal as hot as a blacksmith's hammer. The remaining two walls fall in turn, layering onto each other like a collapsed house of cards. It all falls down.

"This is where I brought my babies home from the hospital," Vi tells us. I know who her babies were: Denny, Lois, and Ron. No matter how many times she may call me *daughter*, we both know. "This is the home I could always come back to."

The fire is down now, and the helpers tame the last flames with the backs of shovels. There is nothing left to burn, only the fuel of memory. The men rake embers into the perimeter of the house. Sparks still rise, like exhausted kids who can't stay in bed because electricity still runs through them.

Finally, the fire settles, contained. Only this footprint remains. The work is done.

ᴉ||ᴦ

Dorothy motions us to her. She holds a bucket of water with sprigs of cedar floating on its surface. "Everyone who witnessed this work here today will need to wash."

Vi goes first. She dips her hands in the water and splashes it on her face. A man hands her a towel, and she holds it to her face and then dries her hands. Drops of rain fall on the last of the burn, on us, and into the bucket.

One by one, we wash. My turn comes, and I slip my hands under the cedar into the cold water, this antidote to fire. I bring my hands to my face. The sting of cold meeting heat. The rough, nubby towel. The helpers go last, and their face paint comes off in the water and on the towel.

Vi thanks Dorothy and her family. We say our goodbyes and get into the car to begin our journey back to Vi's house. We drive past the burn. Vi drops into a silence that isn't really silent. It's that place where songs come from. I lower the window to hear it better, to have one last sense of this place. We see embers, a brick-red glow that marks the house. Like errant fireflies, sparks lift from the embers and rise, carrying the remains of this place. Memories lift like silver ghost smoke up to the sky world, where they will provide a sheltering feast for those on the other side, a feast that will go on long after the night passes and the embers cool.

We drive on. Once we are far enough down the road, Vi speaks. "My mother was telling me this was the only home she ever had. She wanted her house with her. That's why that first fire started. In a lightning storm. Because she wanted it. So today, we just followed what she wanted."

Back at Vi's house, we sit at her table and eat maple-nut ice cream, letting its cold sweetness melt on our tongues and down our dry throats. Vi thanks me with a blanket and thanks Robby with a teddy bear. We take our leave, drive back to Seattle.

At home, at the sink, I wash red clay plates, a teak salad bowl dark with oil, a cast-iron skillet older than our marriage, a knife that has chopped a thousand onions, a much-marked cutting board. I touch these things as if they will always be here. Then I wander to the bedroom and see the blanket and bear, reminders that our home is no more permanent than the one we saw burn. We are all traveling toward the spirit world at speeds unknown. Even at the speed of fire.

Marilyn Wandrey, Vi Hilbert, Bedelia (Samson) Cowen, Janet Yoder, and Robby Rudine at the Nooksack property (photo by grandson Jay Samson)

The house begins to burn at the corners (photo by Jay Samson)

The fire follows the roofline (photo by Jay Samson)

A small flame pops out of the roof (photo by Jay Samson)

The house burns (photo by Jay Samson)

The ritualists push a wall inside the foundation (photo by Jay Samson)

ON TAPE / OFF TAPE

One day for an interview with Vi, I arrive at her home on her daughter's alpaca ranch in Bow on flat Skagit land.

"I woke up at four o'clock this morning to prepare for our work today," Vi tells me. It's the first day of our third interview during Vi's lucid years. She wears a black pareo top with white tropical flowers printed on it. Around her neck hangs a string of shiny black beads, maybe polished ebony.

We take our seats, Vi at the head of her table like the canoe captain, and today I am the only crew. We talk nearly an hour before I can let the tape run. It's protocol, this off-tape time. My old Radio Shack tape recorder and a new ten-dollar microphone sit between us. Finally it's time. I turn on the machine, speak out the date and place, say her name, then mine, and we begin our conversation.

ᔑᖆ

Once she took on the mantle of being the one who stands and speaks Lushootseed, Vi settled in to that role. She spoke in public, telling stories with what appeared to be total ease. She was comfortable being videotaped or filmed, and she is comfortable with my Radio Shack cassette recorder running. She is quite aware of being recorded and wants that. Usually she answers my questions in depth. Once in a while, she shifts the subject. This happened in the previous conversation about her personal life, about her birth, her marriages, and the death of her first son. So we are revisiting her story.

I remind Vi that she told me she was born at Lyman. "Between Lyman and Hamilton," she says. I hear hesitation in her voice. I ask if she was born at home. "Beats me," she says. "I think my mother gave birth all by herself. She was a strong woman. She had to be strong." Something feels odd to me about that, but we move on. I see alpacas enter the field behind the house.

We talk about the man named George Swanaset, who claimed to be her father and was married to her mother when Vi was born. On his deathbed, George Swanaset admitted that Vi was not his daughter. We talk about the man she knows was her real father—Charlie Anderson. He was the true love of Vi's mother. He raised Vi. The hand drum he made now hangs on her wall.

Clouds traverse the sky. Vi's Indian Shaker altar sits in front of the window. A table covered with white cloth. A white wooden cross stands upright in the center, with white candles around it. When the tape is on, I can relax and listen to her soft voice, her speech with lots of pauses. I pull my legs up onto the chair and lean against the back. I let my vision blur because I can hear better that way. I mailed her my questions ahead of time. She had asked for them, though we both know we will wander. The alpacas graze in their field.

Vi tells me how she came to marry her first husband, Percy Woodcock of Quinault. "I was in high school, at Franklin High School in Portland, Oregon. My friend Oma said, *I'm going up to visit my brother in Taholah. Why don't you come with me?* This was when I graduated from high school. I had nothing to do but go home to my mother and dad, and that didn't sound very exciting. So I went with her to Taholah. At that time, she was matchmaking. Her brother was a bachelor. He had a little shack that he had built right by the Quinault River. So we met. He was a very quiet man. Very gentle. He was just there. After a week of visiting with each other and looking at Taholah, he suggested maybe it would be nice if we got married. I was eighteen and just out of high school. I had at that moment no further ambition than to be a wife, a homemaker, and a mother. I thought this seemed like an ideal solution, what a young woman needs to have in her life—a quiet, hardworking man. So, childlike, I said, *Okay.* I married him because he had the qualities that seemed important."

They had a son named Denny and seventeen months later, a daughter named Lois. Vi worked at a café and pool hall and then started her own café, making huge hamburgers to feed her customers—loggers and fishermen—who appreciated the generous good food. She cooked breakfast, lunch, and dinner while a babysitter took care of her children.

Vi's mother came to visit. "My mother saw how hard I was working. She said, *Honey, you can't do all this and take care of your children right. Let me take my grandchildren home.* So my parents took my children home to Nooksack so they could take care of them while I ran my business. After a while, my mother called me and said, *Honey, your son is sick. I think you'd better come home.* So I went home to Nooksack to see my little son. I could tell by looking at him that he had meningitis, because I had worked in a hospital and I'd taken care of a little boy who had meningitis. I could see the symptoms. He went to the hospital. This was before they had any knowledge of how to treat meningitis. He was just burning up with a high, high temperature that just burned him out. He knew at the onset of his sickness that he was contagious. He kept saying, *Don't let my sister get near me.* He said, *God wants me now.* Then he died." After this loss, Vi's first marriage ended. We sit in silence as this loss settles over us.

Vi's cousin Lillian married and moved to Tulalip. Vi visited, and through Lillian, she encountered Bob Coy, a friend from childhood when they attended the Tulalip Boarding School together. "We got acquainted. Bob Coy was fun to be with. He was a good dancer and a good singer. His father was important. He came from a good family. So everything was okay. He was not related, except my folks said he was a fourth or fifth cousin. I said, *Well, that's far enough removed.* As Martin Sampson said, *You did good, cousin. You picked the right men to father your children.* They all come from *si?ab.* Lois's family comes from *si?ab.* Ron's family comes from *si?ab.* I feel very good about that. I picked good fathers to father the children that I had."

On this return trip to her personal life, Vi tells me about how that marriage came unstitched. "He began to drink earnestly. I said to him, *I have two children that I am responsible for, Ron and my daughter, Lois. I will not allow them to endure an alcoholic home. So, I'm going to have you make a choice. If you want to continue drinking, then our marriage is over.* In answer to me, he brought home a case of beer and invited all of his friends to come to our little home. Men and women came. He was a party kid. They loved his company. They came. And while they were all there, I took one bottle after another to the back porch. Down below was a cement deck. I smashed each one of the bottles of beer. One of the women there had a motorcycle. Gas was rationed at that time. I said, *I need to leave here.* So she said, *I have an extra gas coupon.* Some kind person took me and my children and our suitcase back to my cousin Lillian in Tacoma. So I left Bob in my little house that I had paid payments on."

Vi's father asked her to think seriously before ending her marriage to Bob. Vi told him, "He just had to drink more and more. It was endangering the homelife of my children. He got angry once and threw a knife at me. It missed me, thank God, and went through the door. He threw it with such force that had he hit me, it would have gone through my body. So I said to my dad, *I don't take the chance that the next time he throws a knife, it will miss me. Next time he'll hit me.* It was a sickness. I didn't realize that." More silence.

Vi tells me about meeting Don Hilbert, her husband of sixty years. "I met Don when I was living with my cousin Lillian in Tacoma, when we had gone out to this birthday dinner. Don Hilbert was at a table next to ours. He was with a bunch of other Navy men. He kept staring at me. At one point he got brave enough to come over to ask me to dance. My cousin Lil said, *Why don't you dance with him. He has very sad eyes.* So I did. He really couldn't dance at all. After having a dancing partner like Bob Coy, who was a dream to dance with, I thought Don was clutching my body too tightly. I said, *If you don't loosen up, I'm going to walk away from you.* He said, *I'm not being fresh, this is just the way I dance.* I said, *This is not the way you dance with me.* So he loosened up then and we did a few one-two-three slides. So then he said, *I'd like to take you out to dinner.* I said, *Me and my two kids?* He said, *Oh, I love children. Yes. You and your two children.* I said, *I don't think so.* My cousin Lil stepped in again. She said, *Oh, let him come. I'll take care of the kids. You're not going to take your children out to dinner with you.* So he took a cab from Bremerton to Tacoma to take me out to dinner. So that's where the courtship started."

I asked Vi what her parents thought about her marrying outside their culture. "Don could see where my folks needed help. He pitched right in and helped. He showed my dad he was a hard worker. Don and my dad were quiet buddies. My mother was a very spiritual woman. She had ways of seeing into the psyche of another human being. She was a little leery of Don but she always treated him politely."

I ask Vi about her children, if she had a sense when they were young of what they might become. "Oh, heavens yes. The moment they are born, the character is evident. Lois, from the moment she was born, was responsible. Ron was always going to be speaking in a voice that was different from anybody else's. When he started to school, his teacher let me know how they saw him. *Your son needs to be encouraged to do art.*"

I ask how she sees Lois and Ron taking the culture into their adult lives. "Ron indicated to me that he felt that the spirituality of our family needed to be represented. So he decided that he wanted to be the one to do that. So he became an initiate into the longhouse spiritual world that we're a part of. My daughter chose to do other work that was counseling people, to help guide their lives in the ways that she could see was right for them." I will insert here that many times over many years, I have witnessed Lois speaking and telling stories in a way that touches hearts.

I ask Vi whether she imagines the kind of man her firstborn son, Denny, would have become. "Oh, heavens, all the time." Her voice softens. "Because he lives in my heart. And always will. I think that Lois longs for the living spirit of her brother to be with her. He would have been a very strong man, a very beautiful, intelligent man. Because he showed signs of the kind of intelligence that was in him from the time he was born. That precociousness was evidence of what he would be when he grew up. I was so angry at the Creator for giving him to me for such a short time. Finally when I came to terms with the Creator for taking him away from me, I was able to say, *Thank you for allowing me to have him at least three and a half years.* I could just let it go then and be grateful that I had him with me for that long." I hear pure love for this adored son and consider that complexity works its way into families over time.

We drive to the Rhododendron Cafe for lunch. We sit beside green wainscoting with magenta rhododendron wallpaper above. Vi has her glass of Riesling. We order salads, then split an order of curried halibut. I eat slowly. The salad contrasts bitter greens with baby tomatoes as sweet as candy. Curry infuses the halibut.

We finish with coffee. "You know, Janet," Vi says. "I think I might have been born in Canada. My folks were up there visiting relatives, but my dad was Skagit and they wanted me to be American so they told everyone I was born here in Skagit Country."

"Oh?" We have spent most of the morning on Vi's personal life and now this very first fact—the fact of her birth—is in question. I look at Vi and I know she sees openmouthed shock on my face. She smiles. She shrugs. And eventually I smile back at her. We sip our coffee. We are off tape.

Vi Hilbert and Janet Yoder doing an interview (photo by Robby Rudine)

STORY PLACES

NORTH WIND AND SOUTH WIND

North Wind came down to the Duwamish River and he killed South Wind and many of the people who lived there. The wife of South Wind escaped and gave birth to a son. North Wind built a fish weir of ice, which reached across the river and stopped the salmon from running so South Wind's people would die of hunger. North Wind spread ice across the land so that South Wind's people would freeze. But the son of South Wind survived and became South Wind [sometimes known as Stormwind]. His grandfather told him never to go down to North Wind's fish weir. So when he became a man, the young South Wind went down to North Wind's fish weir. He saw all the ice and he found an old woman who lived near the weir. She was his grandmother. She made many baskets and left them outside. South Wind blew, and his warm wind brought rain. When the grandmother's baskets were filled with rain, she poured that rain into the river to flood North Wind's weir. Then South Wind hurled a log at North Wind's frozen ice weir and smashed it. He chased North Wind away. The salmon traveled upriver; South Wind's people had food again and a mild climate.

After North Wind left, what was left of the fish weir he'd built across the Duwamish River was turned to stone. It stretches across the river now. Anybody can see it at low tide when water runs between the stones.

"North Wind" told by Big John (Green River)
and Charles Sotaiakum (Duwamish)

WITH VI AT NORTH WIND'S WEIR

Vi directs us to the Duwamish River to find the place where North Wind's fishing weir—a low handmade dam to trap salmon—blocked the river. Downstream the river has been engineered and straightened; here at the weir, the river is as it was, at least as much as any meandering river is as it was. We step across stones to a little island, all of it part of the storied fishing weir. We stand on the island in the river. The place feels hidden though it's just a home-run hit from a six-story silver-banded Boeing office building and its parking lot. The fishing weir is neither obvious nor easy to get to. You have to know where it is. This is the place where time and story overlap.

THIRTY YEARS LATER

Robby and I return to North Wind's fishing weir thirty years after our first visit with Vi. A Google search shows us where it is, gives us driving directions, and tells us the story. When we arrive, we find Cecil Moses Park with parking for our car. We find a footbridge just above North Wind's fishing weir, artwork depicting the battling North Wind and South Wind as round faces with lines representing air blowing from their mouths. We find a paved trail and see people walking this stretch of river. We find the story Vi told us made visible, accessible to all.

I stand on the footbridge and peer at the murky green-gray river below. Its waters move with the tide, like batter under the churn of a slow-speed mixer, where ingredients mingle and briefly marry in this zone of change, this estuary of salt and fresh with a hint of metal, a thin dredge of sludge, and a pinch of mercury, arsenic, and lead. North Wind's weir appears and disappears daily with the tide.

South Wind has brought us a soft, moist, clement winter day. We walk upriver along a smooth asphalt trail. It is lunch hour and workers from the thriving industries nearby are walking, jogging, biking in fleece vests and GORE-TEX jackets. They talk business or they talk their own stories. This part of the Duwamish is rediscovered, reclaimed. The paved trail passes native planting areas replete with Douglas fir, birch, alder, cedar, ferns, salal, cloudberry bushes, native strawberry trees, and Oregon grape. This part of the river retains its meandering curves. We walk the new trail along this river stirred by sea, rain, and fighting winds, this river that yet carries story.

MOON, THE CHANGER

Two sisters fell in love with two stars and went up to the sky to marry them. One sister had a baby with her star husband. But the sisters were not happy in the sky. They were homesick. They dug a hole in the floor of the sky world and could see the earth below. They wove a rope out of cedar boughs.

The sisters hung the rope down from the sky and found that it reached almost to earth. The younger sister stepped through the hole in the sky to the rope. The elder sister handed the baby to the younger and then stepped onto the rope. She closed the hole in the sky and caused a forest to grow where the sky prairie had been, so that their star husbands, searching, would not be able to find them. Then, when all was ready, the two sisters with the baby descended the rope to earth, their former home.

The news spread that the two sisters had come from the sky. People gathered. The two sisters made the rope into a swing and caused it to swing back and forth. Their father invited the people to have sport and enjoy themselves swinging on the rope his daughters had made.

The baby became Moon, the Changer. Moon said, "The swing will be there forever, and if people wish to go up to the sky, they can get whatever they want." But eventually Rat, who was denied a turn on the swing, gnawed the rope and the swing slipped so the people could not climb to the sky. The swing fell and Rat fell with it. Moon then said, "The people shall now have a swing to have sport upon but it will no longer be so high."

So the people began to swing on the rope between Mount Si and Rattlesnake Mountain. They—especially the bird people— left their big footprints on the sides of the mountains where they pushed off to swing. They did this swing until Moon, the Changer, turned them all into stone. He also turned the swing rope to stone.

"Moon, the Changer" told by Snuqualmi Charlie (Snuqualmi)

WITH VI AT THE SWING ROPE

Jay Miller, Robby, and I travel with Vi across Lake Washington to Snoqualmie Country. We gaze up from I-90 at the large footprints of the bird people scratched into the side of Mount Si, marks made when these giant ones pushed off the side of the mountain to fly across to the other side of the valley. We admire the magnificent scale of these footprints, imagine gigantic bird beings with wingspans of a river.

We meet Greg Watson, director of the Snoqualmie Valley Historical Museum and a Lushootseed volunteer. Together we go in search of the place where the sisters came down to earth, where the swing rope landed. It is a tall boulder that white settlers called Quarry Rock. From one side, it looks like a significant rock, a story place. But when we walk around to the other side, we see this rock has been quarried out. Cars whiz past. Vi talks about how *dukʷibəɬ* (the Changer) began to live on the earth and made things as they are.

THIRTY YEARS LATER

We revisit the place where the swing rope came down. This story place is now overgrown and we would not have found it without the help of Greg Watson, our Lushootseed friend and Snoqualmie scholar. We stand in a patch of stinging nettle under low alder branches. We reach through and touch the rock that in the story was once a cedar branch rope dropping from the sky world. The rock seems smaller. Part of it is on private property and possibly has been quarried more than when we were here with Vi. We know the rock used to be a hundred feet across. We stand in front of the remains. We talk about Rat chewing through the rope and people quarrying through the rock. We reach into our pockets and pull out Sacajawea dollar coins to tuck into moss-covered holes in the rock. We feel the presence of story here.

ᔕᖯ

Story places are all around us. We drive past them on our daily errands. We build on top of them, walk over them, and live right above them. Story places are complex, layered, potent. Think Jerusalem or Constantinople, Rome, Athens, Teotihuacan, Chichén Itzá, Machu Picchu. Some places run deep, down to the soul of the ancients. Some places are so imbued with story that we know it in our bodies, in our deep subconscious. Those

stories find a home in our hearts and teach us how to live in a
particular place on this planet of stories.

Art by Susan Point at North Wind's fishing weir on the Duwamish River,
where North Wind and South Wind battled (photo by Robby Rudine,
used with permission from the artist Susan A. Point)

FINDING SPIRIT

Vi told me about her experience of the Indian Shaker Church. "My mother joined the Indian Shaker Church. At first my father didn't. But she talked to him about the church every day. He just said, *Yes, Mama.* But she kept at it and finally she wore him down. So he joined."

Next I asked Vi about the longhouse and she said, "Later my mother was ill. To get well, she had to sing the song that had come to her and she had to do that in the longhouse. So she entered the longhouse then. She worked on my father again. She knew he had spirit help that had never come out. She wore him down and he entered the longhouse too."

"So, were they still Shakers?"

"Yes. In those days you could belong to both. I think that's harder now."

Vi went on. "So later, my mother joined a Pentecostal church because she could express herself there and she had a big need to express herself."

"Did your dad join too?"

"Of course." Vi laughed. "My mother could get him to do things. She pushed my dad. *Tell your story,* she would say. *Stand up and speak.*" I see where Vi came by her propensity to push those around her to find their work and do their work, then to stand up and speak.

I consider the idea of inclusive spirit, that you could go into the longhouse and still attend the Indian Shaker Church and maybe a Pentecostal church, perhaps also a Catholic church, and nobody forces you to choose one and only one for all time.

Vi's life and her work were guided by spirit.

Vi opened her heart to people of other faiths. She believed there are many paths leading to spirit. At a gathering, I watched her sit with a Buddhist elder, a Hawaiian elder, a Japanese elder, and a Maori elder. With each of these, and with many others she encountered, Vi could find spirit.

Vi Hilbert's mother, Louise Anderson, in regalia
(photo courtesy Lushootseed Research)

Vi Hilbert's father, Charlie Anderson, with Captain, the drum he made
(photo courtesy Lushootseed Research)

Vi Hilbert and Johnny Moses calling on spirit (photo by Paul Eubanks)

Spiritual leaders: Johnny Moses, Bruce Miller, Pauline Hillaire, Vi Hilbert, Isadore Tom, Jewell James, and Kenny Cooper (photo from the collection of Paul Eubanks)

WRAPPED IN A
BLANKET

I knock on Vi's door in the La Conner Retirement Inn. No answer. I knock again and ease the door open. "Hello, *tsi si?ab*," I say. "It's Janet." I hear a mumble and move toward the sound. I peek over the back of the sofa and there is Vi, lying on a blue wool blanket. "Were you sleeping?" I ask.

"No, dear," she says. "Just resting." I bend to give her a kiss. Then I sit near her at the curve of the sectional sofa. I bring my face close to hers and we visit on her blanket. Vi is now eighty-nine. She took a fall a while back and just finished three months of rehab at a convalescent center for fractures to her wrist and collarbone. When I visited her in rehab, she was so diminished it scared me. The pain pills took away her appetite, which wasn't much to begin with.

"We were going to do an interview today, Vi," I say. "Are you still up for that?"

"Sure," she says. But she doesn't move to her recliner where she always sits when we talk.

"Shall we visit right here?" I pat my hand on the blue blanket her head rests on.

"Sure." She smiles at me. The thermostat is set on Hawaii, eighty-five degrees. I slip off my jacket, plug in my Radio Shack recorder, and insert a now-hard-to-come-by cassette tape. I place the microphone on the blue blanket as if setting out a picnic. I test the tape and then hit record.

We review the Lushootseed words. A blanket is sʔičəb or qəlikʷ. A canoe blanket is x̌əč̓ ij̓slucid. A baby blanket is qəliwiʔɬ. A ceremonial blanket is q̓ʷastədulic̓aʔ. A duck down and mountain goat wool blanket is yabdəč̓. A dog wool blanket is statq̓ʷuʔ. A white blanket with a black stripe on each end is təqʷxʷalc.

Vi perks up in response to my questions. "Before there was such a thing as money, our people valued handmade things," she says. "Everyone knew that it took many, many hours for a blanket to be woven. So the gift of a blanket was symbolically an honoring tool. It was more important than money."

᚛᚜

Vi talks about the meaning of blankets in Indian Country. You thank someone with a blanket. You give a blanket to a witness at a naming, one who speaks of what it means to carry a traditional name. You wrap a blanket around a couple getting married. "That blanket is going to be used by two people," Vi says. "It's going to keep them together." Divorce is known as "splitting the blanket."

You present a blanket to an elder to confer honor and express respect. You give a blanket to a person being initiated into the longhouse. Or you give a blanket to a person grieving the loss of a dear one. The blanket spreads protection over someone in a vulnerable time, a time when the spirit world and our world are so close they could kiss.

You might even spread a blanket across a ritual fire to burn it, to send it to your beloved who has passed to the spirit world and will need the blanket's comfort there.

⊓⊩

Weavers were resourceful. Before contact, the First People made blankets of mountain goat wool. In summer, women climbed into the mountains and traversed trails to pluck tufts of wool from bushes on which the goats had shed their coats. Sometimes the wool from now-extinct wool dogs was gathered by young girls and blended with mountain goat wool. Sometimes weavers spun fluff from the ripe seedpods of milkweed, fireweed, or cattail into mountain goat wool. Or threads of nettle, Indian hemp, or pounded cedar. Or animal fur. Or downy bird feathers.

Wool and fiber are spun into yarn using a spindle and whorl. The whorl is a disk with a hole in its center that the spindle goes through. The whorl may be made of wood, stone, shell, or even whale vertebrae. Its job is to keep yarn in place on the spinning spindle and thus maintain the required tension to make yarn. The wool spinner faces the spindle whorl, which may have her spirit help carved into it: wolf, whale, salmon, hawk, eagle, thunderbird, or a human figure whose mouth or heart or stomach is pierced by the spindle. The spindle spins and the whorl whirls, slowly then faster, until the spinner sees her spirit power imbue the yarn with honor for the one who will ultimately wear the blanket.

Spinning is transformational. Look at a whorl without its spindle and this is what you might see: a birth canal, a smoke hole in the roof of the longhouse, a passage between this world and the next.

The Salish loom is a fixed-warp frame made of two upright cedar posts dug into the ground five to six feet apart. Two hardwood crossbars fit into carved slots in the posts. The upper crossbar stays at the top of the frame at a height of around five feet. The lower crossbar is loosened and tightened with wedges. Vertical yarn is the warp, horizontal yarn the weft. Typical Salish weaving styles are *twill*, where the warp and weft threads are both equally visible, and *twine*, where the weft conceals the warp threads.

Weaving was not a chore, nor a casual activity. Weaving was done in winter, during the season of the spirit dance. Just as the spirit dancer must fast, cleanse, and seek spirit help before being initiated, early ethnographers reported that weavers, always women, refrained from sexual relations for two months previous to handling wool for a blanket. These weavers fasted for the first day of wool preparation and fasted again for the first day of weaving.

ᕋᕊ

With the arrival of sheep around 1840, wool became abundant. In 1895, the Pendleton Mill began making blankets for Native Americans. As the fur trade moved west, it brought Hudson's Bay Company Chief's Blankets—white with stripes in green, red, yellow, and indigo, plus small black lines near the edge that tell the size of the blanket. Dollars or furs could buy these wool blankets easier than hands could weave a blanket. People could stack up their wealth in folded wool.

Vi collects blankets before she hosts any event. Her ninetieth birthday is approaching and she shows me what she has gathered: wool blankets from a company in Minnesota, alpaca wool shawls from her daughter, Lois, who raises alpacas, small quilts made by her neighbor at the La Conner Retirement Inn. Some are finer than others and she knows who will receive these.

Vi receives a blanket at every gathering she attends and sometimes she receives three or four. Each blanket—say, a Pendleton blanket depicting the Salmon twins, Raven and the box of knowledge, or the zigzag of Navajo lightning—is lifted up, displayed so everyone can see the pattern. Two people walk behind Vi until the blanket forms a background centered on her. And then they wrap her in the blanket, and Vi stands, majestic in her robe of royalty.

Blankets move around Indian Country. Vi might receive a blanket at one gathering and then present that same blanket to someone else at the next gathering—at Tulalip or Upper Skagit or the Medicine House at Swinomish. Or she might bestow it on a visitor to her apartment if the spirit moves her.

⊐║╠

Vi lies on the blue wool blanket on her sofa, eyes alert. We recall how renowned storyteller Johnny Moses performs a naming by spreading out a blanket on the floor or ground. He has the one receiving a name stand in the middle of the blanket, and the blanket makes a sacred place.

"In the longhouse, if you put a blanket down, then that's your space," Vi says. "Nobody else is going to sit there. You are holding that space for yourself or a member of your family."

We talk about weavers Vi knows. "The Lummi have always been known for their weaving," she says. We talk about Fran and Bill James, who are master weavers at Lummi. "It's usually women that weave," Vi says. "But certain men are drawn to weaving."

⊐║╠

Designers have made clothing out of blankets: vests, coats, hats, and jackets. Vi carries a shoulder bag made of a Pendleton blanket. I have a photo of her wearing a full-length coat made from the Pendleton "Time of Gathering" blanket. In the photo, Vi—resplendent in her blanket coat—offers a snack to a pair of gray jays that hover to eat from her palm. Her blanket coat celebrates one hundred years of statehood for Washington. As I sit with Vi in her apartment in 2008, Washington State is a paltry 119 years old.

Eighth Generation is a Seattle business started by Louie Gong (Nooksack) and now owned by the Snoqualmie Tribe. They offer beautiful blankets as well as scarves, jewelry, towels, mugs, bags, and other items, all designed by Native artists. Their tagline is "Inspired Natives, not Native-inspired." Vi Hilbert's family chose to wrap honored guests in the Coast Salish Pattern wool blanket designed by Louie Gong from Eighth Generation at the dedication of the Vi Hilbert Hall at Seattle University.

ᔅᔅ

I ask Vi about the tradition of cutting blankets into pieces in order to give away those pieces to many people. "Pieces of blanket are shared," Vi says. "So the blanket is not intact, but the sharing means that we're still connected. If you put all the pieces together, you have a full blanket. You have a piece of memory."

ᔅᔅ

After the *Healing Heart Symphony* premiered in Benaroya Hall, after the last notes of the symphony sounded, Vi came out on stage and was wrapped in a blanket. She talked about wanting to complete a documentary about the symphony, a project that required funds. When Vi came out to the lobby wearing her blanket, people pulled money out of wallets and purses and pinned paper money to Vi's blanket. Not just one-dollar or five-dollar bills but tens and twenties, even fifties. Her blanket was covered with money.

Vi stepped out of the lobby and onto the sidewalk by herself to wait for her driver. It was late afternoon and the wind was up. There stood Vi, wearing a blanket covered with currency that quivered in the breeze like butterfly wings. Vi was tiny, maybe weighed ninety pounds. She was eighty-eight years old and nearly blind. And she was covered with cash! Yet, as she stood on Third Avenue in downtown Seattle, no one walking by dared disturb her. No one touched a single dollar on her blanket of wealth.

꼐

Vi was honored with a blanket—a nobility robe—handwoven of mountain goat wool. Skokomish weaver Susan Pavel gathered wool and wove this treasure over years. If the gathering or weaving had taken longer, then we would not have that photo—nor memory—of Vi, wearing this exquisite blanket, appreciating this masterpiece, and giving it value. "It must have weighed fifteen pounds," Vi says. "That's why I was seated when it was wrapped around me." This mountain goat blanket now belongs to the Seattle Art Museum.

"I know that people are very kind and I've received many, many blankets that I honor for a time, and then I pass them on," Vi says. "That's the practice. I think I have given everything away. I pass things on to people who will take good care of the gift. The gifts are passed on. And people know that." If all the blankets Vi ever received were spread out, they might cover a playfield. It would be a beautiful sight to behold. Equally beautiful would be the sight of all the blankets Vi has given.

꼐

You observe the language of blankets. You hear someone say, "This blanket needs to go home with you," as the blanket is wrapped around its recipient. You understand the blanket has spoken, and you wonder whether you will ever hear a blanket speak.

Vi invites you to enter her world—the world of the First People—just a little. You know you will always be of the second people, the late arrivers on the scene. You know you are only in Vi's world enough to get an inkling of how to live in this place where the First People have lived so much longer.

In 1992, exactly five hundred years after Columbus arrived, Vi holds a quincentennial gathering at the Seattle Art Museum. You settle at a table just outside the auditorium. You have edited a book about Vi, written by her friends and relatives. You spread the books across the table. The cover of the book hosts a photo of Vi wearing a traditional blanket woven by Fran and Bill James of Lummi. The photo is letterpress printed, debossed into card stock. You run your finger across the book's cover and feel the texture of Vi's blanket.

At the Seattle Art Museum, you are sparked up. You give books to Vi, to Vi's friends and family, to the people in her world. You have done your work. It is time to enter the auditorium.

You sit in the auditorium. This museum holds a cedar bark dress that belonged to Vi, baskets that belonged to her, and work by her son Ron Hilbert. Vi's gifts are making this museum rich.

You listen to the Tulalips sing their power song, the one they sing in the longhouse, the one they sang when this new art museum in downtown Seattle was dedicated. The song finishes and Vi steps up to the microphone. She balances the Columbus quincentennial by speaking in Lushootseed—a language older than English—and by telling stories from the time when animals were people.

You watch Vi hold up the book. You are afraid Vi will call you up on stage to thank you, even as you know Vi will call you up on stage to thank you. She calls your name. You are light-headed, but you rise and walk to the stage. You receive a hug from Vi. Now in her hands is a blanket. It is not a Pendleton blanket, not a Hudson's Bay blanket. It is a handwoven blanket made by the Lummi weaving stars. Vi wraps this thick blanket around you. She hugs you again. You cry. Of course you cry. Vi has wrapped you in a woven treasure and you know what it means. You will be warm for life.

You stand on the stage. Vi nudges you toward the microphone. You look out at the people gathered and see many who have contributed to the book. You look down at the beautiful blanket you are wearing. For a second you wonder if it is the same blanket Vi wears on the cover of the book. You have no words. You pull words out of your heart, words of deep gratefulness, though you cannot now remember those words. You leave the stage changed, as if you have passed through the hole at the center of the spindle whorl. You touch the wool and feel its blessing.

You go home at the end of the day and you spread this blanket over the bed you share with your husband. You pull this blanket over you, and you feel as if you have done one good thing, one thing you were meant to do.

You learn to give a blanket to your nephew and his bride, wrap it around them as they celebrate their marriage. You learn to thank your beloveds with a blanket, as Vi has thanked you.

You cover yourself with this blanket and you understand it is not really yours. You know when the time comes, it is your job to wrap this blanket around your chosen one in the way that Vi wrapped it around you.

Weaving masters Bill James and Fran James wearing the Pendleton "Time of Gathering" blanket with Vi Hilbert at the Burke Museum (photo by Kenneth Greg Watson)

Janet Yoder wraps Vi Hilbert in a blanket, with Robby Rudine to Vi's right (photo courtesy Chris Leman and EastlakeInfo.Net)

ON THE OUTS

Vi was angry with me once. Not stomp-your-feet-and-curse angry. She was disappointed in me. Here is how it came about: Vi did lots of projects and I was one of her volunteer helpers on nearly all of those projects. But when she proposed Lushootseed Theater, where we were each to become one of the animals that were people in the legends and act out those legends while being videotaped, I decided that was one project I could miss. We had just gotten a puppy, a fuzzy girl named Saba who needed to pee once an hour because she had a puppy-sized bladder. So I told Vi I wasn't going to be involved in Lushootseed Theater. I was going to stay home with our puppy. I told her over the phone, sitting on our sofa at our houseboat, with Saba on my lap. I heard Vi's voice shift, heard her speech become formal. I froze. Suddenly I knew I was on the outs with Vi. We said goodbye. The day came, and my husband, Robby, went off to Lushootseed Theater and I stayed home with Saba.

A month passed, a month of feeling the loss of Vi, the loss of being in her world along with the rest of her Lushootseed family, the loss of being in the right place, even the loss of the part of myself that came from being with Vi. I knew then how someone who is shunned by her community must feel.

The time came for Robby and me to host a long-planned meeting for Lushootseed Press at our office. Vi arrived. She said hello but she did not open her arms to give me a hug as she had always done before. This left me shaken. We all sat in a circle. After we had admired the new Lushootseed font, after we had reviewed the layout for the book of Aunt Susie's stories and chosen its cover, after we had discussed the finances of publication, after we had taken on our assignments, after we had drunk coffee and eaten French pastry, Vi thanked us all. As she prepared to leave, she gave me a hug. It wasn't a full Vi hug, but I knew I was on my way back into her world.

I remember how easily Vi could cut someone off. A woman in Vi's circle volunteered to edit the Lady Louse stories that Vi had collected from each student who took her Lushootseed literature class or from listeners who took up her challenge to write their own Lady Louse story. This woman took the box of papers home and—according to Vi—stuck it in a corner and left it there. Ironic, since the original Lady Louse story is about Lady Louse finally cleaning her great big house, which was very dirty. This woman let the box sit in her house for a year, maybe two years, until Vi got angry and asked her to return the Lady Louse stories. Once Vi had them back, I volunteered to edit the book for her and I was prepared to get it done pronto.

The thing about Vi was that you could not discuss a speculative idea with her. If you brought up any project idea or any idea at all with her, she interpreted the conversation to mean you had just volunteered to do that project. She then told everyone she knew that you were going to do it. For example, Vi wanted to have a cultural center on the Skagit River where she grew up to house her significant archive. She wanted it to be a place where people—especially tribal people—could access recordings of their ancestors, books, documents, photographs, videos.

A property in Lyman came on the market and Vi went to see it. But it was in a lowland right along the river, a place prone to floods. We were discussing this challenge. Robby asked, "What if we made a floating cultural center?" We live on a floating home on Lake Union and know about flotation and moorings to a lake whose level changes each spring and fall. So Robby floated the idea of building a floating structure. Later I heard Vi tell someone, "Robby Rudine is going to build me a floating cultural center on the Skagit River." Robby had to sort that out with Vi and then become more careful about tossing around ideas.

Later Vi decided she would get a motor home that would be a mobile cultural center that she and anthropologist Jay Miller would travel around in, sharing the culture. However, Jay Miller had no intention of joining Vi in this idea. She likely stopped speaking to him for a while then. That happened a few times during their years of close collaboration.

A friend of Vi's named Carolyn once lived on the Big Island of Hawaii for over a year. Vi arrived to visit Carolyn for a month and they had a grand time together. After Carolyn returned to live in Seattle, the two of them traveled to Hawaii together a number of times. Later still, when Carolyn wanted to travel to Hawaii on her own, she could not mention her travel plans in front of Vi or there would be a rift.

We all loved Vi. We admired Vi. We learned from Vi. We wanted to work with Vi. We wanted to be in her world. But we all knew her expectations were sometimes greater than we might be able or willing to meet. Still, the closest I have felt to knowing I was in the right place was sitting at Vi's dining table in the house she and her husband built on Des Moines Way South, looking out the east window at her well-stocked bird feeder, drinking strong French-roast coffee, and visiting. Vi was not perfect, but being in her world was as close as I could get to having everything right. Being briefly estranged let me know that. Vi and I patched it up. She welcomed me back and we became closer after that.

As an elder, Vi felt the urgency to get her work done. This meant she was not always patient with us younger, slower helpers with other needs and desires to fulfill. But if I could, I would jump up this instant, drive to her house, and sit down at her table for one more visit with Vi.

Vi Hilbert and Janet Yoder (photo by Robby Rudine)

ELVIS SINGS AND
WE TALK OF LOVE

I am driving Vi in her car, coming home from Swinomish. We have the road and a stretched-out summer evening in front of us. Vi inserts her cassette of Elvis love songs. Who knew that Vi, the queen of Lushootseed, was in love with the king who loves us tender, loves us true. Does that tremolo in his voice evoke the truth about love? Or does Vi just decide to tell me a story?

"You know, Janet, Don was in love before I met him," Vi says. "His first love, Lily, sent him a 'Dear John' letter while he was in the Navy. That was kind of mean." I look at Vi and see a look on her face that I have not seen before. Is it hurt? Anger? "So he was on leave. My cousin Lillian and her husband helped me find a babysitter and took me out for an evening. Don was there in his Navy uniform. Handsome. He was looking at me for a long time. Finally he asked me to dance."

Elvis moves on. He just can't help falling in love with us. "The first thing I told him was that I have two kids at home. So he invited me and my kids out to dinner."

"That was a good sign," I say. I am finding Elvis compelling. Emotion rises right through his voice and through the song, like water gurgling up through a hard-crust earth.

"Of course he's hardly taken me out for dinner since then." Vi reaches for a cup and pumps some of her strong black coffee from the thermos that accompanies her on every trip into Indian Country. She sips. We are on a two-lane road passing through flat Skagit Delta farm country. Corn, alfalfa, cabbage. Green in every direction. "Don got word from his sister that Lily's husband had died. Don told me this."

"Oh, when was this?"

"Just a few years ago," Vi says. "So I told him he could go see her and find out if he was still in love with her."

"Oh, Vi. You didn't."

"I did," she says.

"But he didn't go," I say.

"He went," Vi says. Elvis has paused between songs.

I don't know what to say. Finally I ask, "What happened?"

"He came back and told me he wasn't in love with Lily anymore."

"Of course he wasn't," I say.

"Dear, the problem is that when he came back, I wasn't in love with Don anymore. I don't play second best." Elvis promises to make the world go away.

"But Don didn't love Lily," I say.

"He didn't know that when he left," Vi says. "And neither did I."

The sun rides low in the western sky, and the Olympic Mountains stand out in jagged silhouette. I feel sad and shaken. Many of us in Vi's world believe that we stand on the bedrock of Vi and Don's marriage, of their hospitality, the home they made together.

"But Don does so much for you," I say. "He drives the motor home up to the longhouse, he helps you host gatherings, he teaches the grandkids how to garden, how to dig clams. He's a good man."

"Yes," Vi agrees. "Don is a good man. There is just no romantic love between us. Not like you and Robby."

"Well, Vi, Robby is not always romantic."

"But I saw how he treated you on Valentine's Day." Robby and I had once taken Vi to lunch on Valentine's Day at a café near the Pike Place Market. Flowers on the table, French food, then buttery berry tarts in the shape of hearts. Robby was charming. Vi was charmed. "Don has never done a thing for Valentine's Day."

"But Valentine's Day is not the measure of a marriage, Vi," I say. "Anyway, Robby and I had rough times in our early years." Vi looks at me. I hesitate to speak because I know she adores Robby. And I adore Robby. Elvis can't stop loving us. "The first decade of our relationship was kind of crazy, Vi."

"Yes," she says. "I knew something of that."

"We each had other relationships," I say. "We both dated other people, even when we were together."

"Oh," Vi says.

"It was messy and we hurt each other. Robby and I were engaged back then, Vi," I say. "We set a date. Then we broke up and canceled the date. We had to tell everyone. We went to Deception Pass on the day we were meant to marry. We cried. Then we separated. For three years."

"Oh," Vi says. I can tell she did not know all of this.

"Robby lived with a woman named Rose, and I moved to Portland and lived with a man named Meredith. It did not look like Robby and I would ever be back together." I recite a flash-card version of our years apart, though those years were anything but a flash card.

"But the Creator didn't mean for you to be with the others. The Creator drew you back together."

"Yes, Vi," I say. "But it took us a long time and a lot of tears to figure out what the Creator meant for us to do."

"But you ended up together," she says.

"Yes," I say, "we did. So did you and Don." Vi is trying to mend my past and I am trying to mend her present.

"But not in the same way," Vi says. "Don doesn't have a romantic bone in his body."

"Romance isn't everything, Vi."

"It is if you don't have it." Elvis asks if we are lonesome tonight. "That's why I tell people I am going to take eight lovers."

"Right," I say. "I know you like to say that. You like to shock people."

"But you understand what I'm saying, dear. Not sexual lovers. But romantic lovers."

I nod. I do understand. We are driving into and right through Seattle. Buildings lit. Magenta sky. Olympic Mountains fully dimensional. Layers of purple ridges and deep valleys, each its own watershed feeding its own river of stories. These mountains remind us that there is more than meets the eye. There is a whole range of mountains and a whole ocean beyond. We can go there with a full tank of gas, an endless summer evening, and desire.

But we don't go to the mountains. Nor to the ocean. We go to Vi's house on Des Moines Way South and park in her curved driveway with wisteria hanging over it. Elvis needs our love tonight but we turn off the engine. Silence. We stay in the car and finish our talk. Then I walk her into her house and give Don a hug.

Don & Vi
Colorado Springs, Colo
July, 1947

Don and Vi Hilbert in 1947 (photo courtesy Lushootseed Research)

Don and Vi Hilbert in 1996 (photo courtesy Lushootseed Research)

VI'S MEMORY
IS HER TREASURE

Vi's knowledge of her language and culture was her treasure. It lived in her memory. Vi Hilbert could connect Lushootseed back to childhood, to hearing her folks speak the language to each other. Vi found she remembered what most others could not. Her memory served her well for decades of work preserving, publishing, and teaching Lushootseed.

In the last years of his life, Vi's husband, Don, began forgetting things, slipping in and out of a fog that at first was thin as a mist. But the fog thickened and made it hard for him to find his familiar memory pathways. Don got nervous. He sometimes lost his way with names of people, even people he knew well. He couldn't call up his memory. He laughed and shrugged but his eyes showed fear. Vi witnessed this loss every day and it made her impatient with Don. She wanted to distance herself from him as if his memory loss were a contagious disease.

Vi wanted to move back to Seattle to work her mind. "I need to get back in harness," she said. "I have work to do." Her work was exercising her memory, a memory younger minds only dream of. Those younger minds studied what Vi knew, making textbooks, flash cards, lesson plans, videos. Vi offered what she remembered and others took it up. They followed patterns and word order, identified the root, prefix, and suffix. They worked the words, sounds, meanings, stories, place names, plant names, people's names.

After her second aneurism and surgery for it in 1985, Vi went at her Lushootseed work with new vigor and new urgency. Her speech was different. She paused more. I had the impression she was working twice as hard to do memory's work. She was driven. Impatient. If an aneurism was a warning that her time on this earth was limited, it was perhaps a more dire warning that her memory could be limited. As she often said, she needed to get the work done while "everything was on the platter," while she lived in her enumerated lucid years.

She became Ant in the story of Bear and Ant. She tightened her belt and went to work, day and night, day and night. She could not afford to hibernate like Bear did. The speed of her work ratcheted up. She made her coffee stronger. She became bossy. She pushed herself and others to complete the work.

But an elder's memory can change, even a good memory. Vi used to tell any number of stories, even long stories. Then in her later years, she told only two or three stories. Later still, she told only one. I remember sitting at Elliott Bay Book Company, listening to Vi tell the Lady Louse story. She wandered off the story thread. She began to simply talk to her audience. I sat beside her daughter, Lois, whose body tensed as her mother's story wandered. Those of us who knew Vi and knew the story held our breath, fearing that she was lost. Perhaps she was briefly. But she came back in the end, brought it around in a way that deepened the story. She did not—like Lady Louse—get truly lost.

During her lucid years, Vi began giving away her baskets, special blankets, dentalium and "Happy Bead" necklaces, and cedar bark bolo ties. But she clung to her memory, her one true treasure.

Vi Hilbert telling stories (photo courtesy Lushootseed Research)

CARRYING A NAME

Summer. Saturday. 1985. Robby and I drive to Vi's house. She greets us at her door with her arms open. We gather her tote bag and thermos, get her settled up front in our red Subaru station wagon. Then we head north on Interstate 5. Vi pours us triple-strength, black-as-night French-roast coffee from her thermos. She passes around a ziplock bag of sliced peeled apples, then another bag of roasted cashews. We arrive in La Conner and cross the Rainbow Bridge to the Swinomish Reservation. Past the tribal offices, past the Catholic church, Vi directs us up through woods and then off to the right onto a dirt road toward an old unpainted Indian Shaker church. Here we will witness a naming.

We park. Two men stand near the cedar plank building. When they recognize Vi, they come to greet her and help her out of the car. They shake our hands and guide us around to an open space behind the church. A fire burns in a large area surrounded by stones. People gather around the fire. We join them.

This is how Vi Hilbert received the name *taqʷšəblu* (TAWKW-shuh-blue): "So I was visiting my cousin Minnie Johnson, and she was taking care of this ancient old lady and this old lady's husband. Their bedroom was in the living room of Minnie's house at Deming. There was a big potbelly stove there. I was running around doing what a three-year-old would do. I was getting on their nerves, those old people. So *cisłat̓ʔal* said, *taqʷšəblu, stop what you're doing. Stop what you're doing.* She kept calling me *taqʷšəblu.* And so I turned to Minnie and I said, *Make her quit calling me that dog's name.* And Cousin Minnie said, *It's not a dog's name, you crazy thing. That's your name.*"

⊓⊏

A short, dark-haired woman stands between the fire and a blanket spread on the ground with plates of food on it. "That's Mary Bill from Canada," Vi tells us. "She is the ritualist for the burning." We watch as Mary Bill lifts a paper plate with salmon, potatoes, and Jell-O on it. She speaks a name and then places the plate on the fire. Flames work around the edge of the plate, burn through the paper, and eat through the food. Other plates hold more food: spaghetti, a hamburger, blackberry pie, applesauce, Oreo cookies. For each plate offered to the fire, a name is spoken. Mary Bill pours a cup of coffee onto the fire, then a bottle of Pepsi. She speaks more names, places a sweater and a baseball cap on the fire. Then a guitar. The guitar strings pop in the heat. Empty now, the blanket reveals its blue field with stripes in red, yellow, and green. Mary Bill shakes the blanket out, lets it sail across and then float down over the entire fire, like a quilt over a bed. The blanket subdues the fire. Then smoke seeps around the edge of the blanket, and after a while smoke works through the thick weave.

The burning is finished, the spirits named and fed. Mary Bill takes a bucket of water in one hand and a cedar branch in the

*other. She swishes the cedar through the water then brushes it
over the head of the woman next to her. People line up to be
cleansed with cedar and water.*

᠉

Chief William Shelton of Snohomish tells us that the Changer—
dukʷibəɬ—came from the east. This powerful one traveled west
to name the world. He carried a basket full of languages, names
for everything. The Changer arrived at salt water and still had
lots of languages left, so he tossed his basket in the air, and the
words scattered like duck down. That's why we have so many
languages around here. So many names.

Giving names is a power. The word for a traditional healer—
dxʷdaʔab—holds the root word for *name*. Open a map of Puget
Sound, and you will see Lushootseed names—the names
of places, which are also the names of the people who live in
those places: Duwamish, Suquamish, Snohomish, Snoqualmie,
Swinomish, Stillaguamish, Tulalip, Puyallup, and Skagit, to
name a few.

᠉

*Now we step through the door. A woman greets us and pins a
ribbon about five inches long on Vi as if she has won first place
at the fair. She pins a ribbon on me, then Robby. I look down and
see letters spell a name vertically down the ribbon. Before we
find our seats, we each wear two more ribbons, two more names.
Names to be given and received today.*

᠉

Parents name children at birth, sometimes a popular name like
Britney or Caitlin, sometimes an ancestor's name like John

Thomas III, which becomes JT, Buddy, Skip, or Chip. We name children, dogs, cats, cars, companies, rock bands, boats, ranches, songs, poems, and iPhone apps. We give love names or nicknames that suggest intimacy or affection, like the friends of Bill Gates who call him Trey.

A chef names a new dish made of partridge, pomegranate, and pistachio. A rose breeder names his new hybrid with petals the color of papaya. An astronomer names the comet that she is first to track across the night. Fiction writers name a whole world of people and places. Think William Faulkner and Yoknapatawpha County, Gabriel García Márquez and the town of Macondo, or the Herman Melville opening, "Call me Ishmael."

My grandmothers were Hazel and Gladys. My great-aunts were Clover, Kate, and Agnes. My mother is Elsie. Some heirloom names are coming back around. For tomatoes too. Just root them in rich earth, water them, and give them sun. Soon your vines will yield Green Zebras, Jubilees, Early Girls, Brandywines, Cherokee Purples, Hillbillies, and Mortgage Lifters.

ᚾᛁᚱ

Inside the cedar plank house, folding chairs are set up at one end facing an altar that holds a white cross, white candles, and two brass handbells. Vi is led to a seat up front. We take seats in the back. A man calls three children forward, a girl around thirteen and two boys a bit younger. They look like siblings. The man speaks, thanks each and every person in the room for being present. He talks about the names these three are about to receive. "All of us here will be the ones to help them carry those names with honor."

ᚾᛁᚱ

1990. Robby and I plan a slender building for our office, in part to house Lushootseed work. We take our architect, Zen McManigal, to meet Vi. He brings a Styrofoam-board model that rises up from its foundation in the shape of a chief's copper. Vi considers the skinny building set on its Styrofoam slope. Four floors: one home or office on each floor. In turn, Vi shows us a cedar wood model of a longhouse. We discuss. By the end of the evening, Vi gives our building its name: *xʷaac ʔalʔal* ([Whats-ALL-all] Elevated House). "It was the name given to an important house on Nookachamps Creek, a tributary of the Skagit River," Vi says. "People who know the culture will recognize the name and know it is a respected name." She nods approval of her choice. "And Kenny Moses will do the naming ceremony."

1992. Sunshine. The elevated house is finished. Kenny Moses arrives on the appointed day with his extended family—wife, daughter, son, and grandkids—two hours early. He knows Vi expects people to come early. I offer beverages. They drink Cokes. Kenny Moses speaks softly with us. Then Vi arrives. Her husband, Don, carries her big video camera. Her son Ron is there too, ready to see his cedar carving receive its blessing. We gather in front of the garage, above which is Ron's carving, covered with red cloth that runs twenty-six feet across the width of the building, like a giant red headband.

Kenny's people pull drums out of cloth bags. Kenny sings and his family backs him up. People move in close. Ron pulls away the red cloth to reveal the carved and painted world of a longhouse and three salmon stories flanked by Mount Rainier and Mount Baker. Below is a line written in Lushootseed from Chief Seattle's speech that reads, "At night, when the streets of your cities and villages fall silent, and you think them deserted, they will throng with the returning hosts that once filled and still love this beautiful land."

We enter the building and climb the stairs to the top floor. We gather there in the high-ceilinged living room of this home.

Kenny steps forward to speak and sing and pray. He is strong and no longer soft-spoken. He blesses the gathering and gives the building its name: *xʷaac ʔalʔal*. We stand in this elevated house above Lake Union, an echo of that previous elevated house near the Skagit River where Vi grew up. The name links us to that ancestor house that exists no longer. Perhaps that is why its name can be given. We strive to live up to that first Elevated House.

⊐⌐

I watch the three young people. The man in charge speaks each name as if calling to someone far away. He lets the names hang in the air. Then the elders—including Vi—address the gathering. The kids do not fidget. What are they thinking as they stand there, hearing elders talk about carrying a traditional name? Do they wonder if the name will help them? Or worry whether they are up to the responsibility? People have gathered, including elders who likely knew the ancestors who carried the names being given today.

⊐⌐

2010. My dear friend Carolyn Michael and I visit Vi's great-granddaughter Sasha in Santa Fe, New Mexico. We sit across from each other on the lush patio of the India Palace, eating saag paneer and chicken tikka masala.

Sasha wears a nose ring, multiple earrings, and a silver sunray necklace that looks designed for Navajo royalty. She has an array of tattoos across her shoulders and chest and down her arms. Her mood or the weather determines what she reveals.

Sasha rests her arms on the table, and there on her forearm—in red ink—is the name *taqʷšəblu*. It is new since last I saw Sasha. Since Vi passed away. "Look at your tattoo." Sasha holds her arm up for my friend Carolyn and me to admire. Healers in the longhouse wear red paint. Warriors wear black. Vi's family wore red paint. Her son Ron wore red paint. Now Sasha wears the name—her name—in red ink. The name penetrates layers of skin, making it as permanent as her arm.

Sasha, a student at the Institute of American Indian Arts, has a whole lifetime of carrying her ancestor's name on her arm and in her heart. I know that Sasha will speak the name when she introduces herself. The name—*taqʷšəblu*—will remind her always who she is. I look at Sasha and I see Vi standing behind her and then I see Vi's ancestors standing behind her, and an infinite line back. I am in awe of this strong young woman who now carries this ancient name.

Speakers give their words of advice to the young ones. When the last words are spoken, the three children walk around the room to shake hands with every witness. I shake one boy's hand and speak his new name, then the next boy. Both look down and say thank you. The girl's hand feels like feathers. Her eyes are as full and dewy as a bride's. She is now joined with her ancestor's name.

A traditional name moves down from past to present to future. The name is always old and always new. If you look at the Treaty of Point Elliott signed in 1855, you will see high-status Indian names, traditional names. Likely those exact same names are carried today and will be carried a hundred years from today by people not yet born.

Vi's nephew Johnny Moses likes to tell this story: A Catholic priest came west until he found an Indian. The priest taught the Indian the ways of the Catholics. The priest baptized this Indian and named him James. Later, on a Friday, the priest arrived to find the Indian eating venison. The priest said, "James, I taught you not to eat meat on Fridays." The Indian said, "It's all right, Father. I baptized this deer and named him Fish."

⊐∥ℾ

Gifts are given, prayers offered, and Indian Shaker Church songs sung. Platters full of king salmon, venison, potatoes, and fruit pass hand to hand. We fill our plates and eat food prepared for the living—Indian comfort food—to sustain our memories of this day.

⊐∥ℾ

I confess that I do not now recall the three names given that summer day to children—now adults nearing forty—at Swinomish. But I remember the fresh flush on the faces of the three chosen children as they joined the ranks of those who carry a traditional name; I remember the pride and approval on the faces of the elders who had carried their names near a lifetime.

⊐∥ℾ

We gather ourselves back into the car. We make our leave in the late afternoon in golden light. We drive back to our city named for a great Duwamish/Suquamish chief, past the University of Washington where we first met Vi, past Lake Union—miʔmaṅ x̌ačuʔ—"Little Lake," past the Space Needle, past Seattle's shiny downtown—dᶻidᶻ'alal'ič—"Little Crossing-Over Place," and south to Vi's house. We thank her for inviting us, and we

*speak her traditional name—taqʷšəblu—and the name sounds
ancient and present, ephemeral and enduring, a big name to
carry.*

ᗞᖮᗡ

I consider names. I consider my name. A web search reveals
that my first name means "God is gracious" and my last name
evolved from Theodorus, which means "gift of God." I wonder
if I am up to carrying this godly name. But it is my name, and
each of us has a name. All we can do is take up our name and
carry it forward with whatever honor we can muster for our span
of years.

Four generations: Vi Hilbert, Jill La Pointe, Sasha La Pointe, Lois Dodson
(photo by Carolyn Michael)

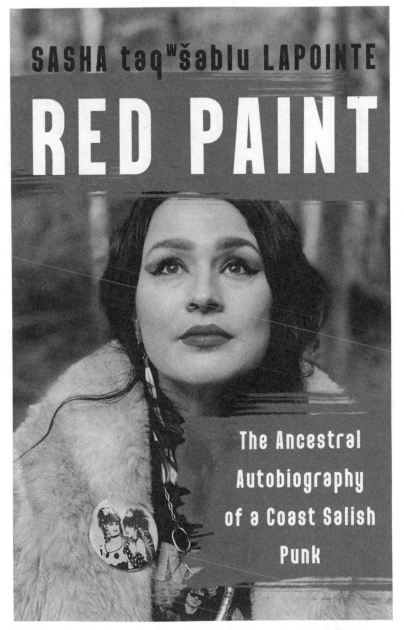

The cover of Red Paint *by the new taqʷšəblu* (photo courtesy Sasha La Pointe)

LOST AND FOUND

Vi told me once about seeking out an elder in Indian Country to help her with her research. Vi arrived at the elder's home, sat, and visited about everyone they both knew, as protocol requires. Then she set up her tape recorder, hit record—or at least she thought she hit record—and began asking her questions of this elder who might remember more Lushootseed than Vi did. Back at home, she played the tape and found it was blank. She lamented the loss and then sat down to write what she remembered.

Later Vi was collecting as many versions of the traditional stories as she could find. She said, "One of my relatives was a blind man and he was a very good listener. People loved to tell him stories because he was such a quiet and good listener. He listened to many, many storytellers and he remembered the way they told a story. Then he would repeat the way they told the story, a little piece and another little piece. And sometimes he didn't remember the way a story was told in what was considered a proper form. People knew that he had taped himself doing these stories. But because they were not told in proper form, the elders gathered up all those tapes and burned them. I was so disappointed. But it's gone. It's gone. And I can't get it back."

ᗆᒷ

Early in her Lushootseed work, Vi came into the mother lode of Lushootseed material: the tape recordings made by Leon Metcalf during the early 1950s. "Oh, I know how lucky I am," Vi said. "I'm so lucky to have had that wonderful volunteer scholar, Leon Metcalf, record some of the oldest of our voices."

Vi was tenacious in getting a copy of the written work that anthropologist Sally Snyder had done with Vi's mother and father. Vi described how she tracked down that material in one of our interviews as follows:

"Years went by and I had not received copies of what I knew had been promised to me. So I went in search of information. I went in search of answers. If a promise is made, I expect a promise to be kept. So I told Pam Amoss [anthropologist, dear friend, and Vi's adopted sister] about the things that had been promised to me and asked how I could go about getting them. Pam said, *It was Sally Snyder who worked with your parents.* I said, *How do I contact Sally Snyder? Well, she was the student of Mel Jacobs,* she said. *How do I find this man?* I asked. *There is going to be an anthropology conference in Seattle, at one of the big hotels,* she said. *Sally Snyder will be there. Margaret Mead will be there. Mel Jacobs will be there.*

"I had a full thriving hairdressing schedule at that time, but I got in my car and drove to the conference to seek out Sally Snyder. I said, *You worked with my parents. You interviewed my parents. They told me that you promised to make copies available for me of the things they told you.* I said, *I haven't received those. Oh, Mel Jacobs has them,* she said. *Where is he?* I asked her. *He'll be here.* I said, *I want to meet Mel Jacobs.* We found Mel Jacobs and I said, *I understand that you have the Sally Snyder material that was promised to me. No,* he said. *I don't have that.* Sally Snyder said, *Oh, yes you do, Mel. It's in your office. In my office? Yes, it's in your office, Mel.* I said, *Where is your office, Dr. Jacobs? At the University of Washington,* he said. I said, *Let's go.* He said, *I don't have a car.* I said, *I do. I will take you.* So I rounded up Mel Jacobs and Sally Snyder and we went to the university.

"We went to Mel's office. Sally opened a drawer in his file cabinet and she said, *The material is right here, Mel.* He said, *Oh, you're right, Sal.* I said, *I want a copy of that. Well, I can't do that,* he said. *It was promised to me. I want a copy of that.* He said, *I'll have Pam Amoss make you a copy and deliver it.* I said, *I expect a promise to be kept.*

"So Pam Amoss had been working with my parents and she said, *I'm going to make you a copy of the material that Sally did with your folks.* So Mel let her have a copy of that, because he didn't trust dumb Indians like me to take good care of information. I don't blame him. I don't blame him at all. He was just being careful. But I had to insist on getting a copy of that material." (Vi recounts this story somewhat differently and at greater length in Jay Miller's books, *Rescues, Rants, and Researches: A Review of Jay Miller's Writings on Northwest Indien Cultures* and *Herstories Northwest: Women Upholding Native Traditions.*)

⊓⌐

After such effort, it is understandable that Vi lamented the loss of any Lushootseed material. Here is how she recounted such a loss:

"One of my relatives, a very spiritual man, was preaching over the radio, preaching in the language every Sunday. I could turn on the station and hear him. That was such a wonderful treat to me, to hear somebody doing what I had heard all my life, hearing my people praying in church in the language. Because they didn't know English, they only knew Lushootseed. They prayed that way. I realized that this relative who was preaching in the language was on tape. All those tapes were at this radio station in Everett, Washington. So I tried to investigate whether copies would be available. The management had changed hands and they had destroyed all those tapes. I was so disappointed and angry because that resource had been snatched away."

꩜

How do we track down what is most precious to our people, to our culture, whatever culture that may be? How do we preserve what we find—photographs, recordings, stories, teachings, histories, songs? How do we share what we find? Do we write books, produce CDs or podcasts, put information on websites, maybe on Ancestry.com? Vi would say yes. A big emphatic yes!

꩜

Here is my confession: I interviewed Vi many times. Each time, I set up my old Radio Shack tape recorder, put in a tape, and did a sound test. Then I hit record. In the last few interviews, side A of each tape had recorded perfectly, but side B recorded not at all. Nothing at the beginning, nothing in the middle, and nothing at the end. I took those few tapes into the audio lab at the University of Washington School of Ethnomusicology. Even their best geeks could not retrieve anything from side B.

I was devastated. This happened during the last year of Vi's life, just after her ninetieth birthday. Her energies were failing. After lamenting the loss, I sat down to transcribe side A and then write what I remembered of side B—the second half of our conversation.

꩜

Perhaps there is always loss as we make our way, find our material, and do our work. Computers crash, tape recordings turn up blank, degrade, or get destroyed, videotapes go missing, even social media posts can be deleted. In the end we go back to our memory. Vi was blessed with the fine material she tracked down and worked on, preserved for the future. And she was equally blessed by her memory. She knew Lushootseed and she knew how the language meshed with the way her people treated each other, meshed with the rivers that flow through this part of the world, meshed with spirit, with stories of the animals, of the Changer, of how things came to be as they are in this beautiful place. Vi made certain this would not be lost.

Mel Jacobs and Pamela Amoss (photo likely by Vi Hilbert, courtesy Lushootseed Research)

BASKET SONG

There is a story told by Kenny Cooper of Lummi about a young girl who wants to become a basket weaver. One of the elder women of her village teaches the girl how to gather cedar bark, saying a prayer before taking a strip of bark from this sacred tree. She shows her how to take the inner bark from the strip, how to pound it, shred it, and ready it for weaving.

Under the elder's guidance, the young girl crafts her first basket. The girl's attempt is clumsy. The basket is loose; the weave has openings that light shines through. The girl shows it to her teacher. The elder tells the girl, *Go down to the river and fill your basket with water. Then carry it back to me.* The girl goes down and fills the basket, but the water flows out through the loose weave, splashing right back into the river.

The girl returns with her empty basket, and the elder tells her to start again. The girl does as she is asked. She makes a second basket with a tighter weave. Less light comes through. But the river water still flows out, if perhaps a little slower. Her teacher tells her to start again.

The young girl's third try is tighter. This time, the river water only drips out. The girl knows what she must do.

Her fourth try is right. The weave cinches together so that the basket is strong and tight. This time, water stays in the basket, and the elder compliments the girl for weaving such a fine basket.

Before the girl can take pleasure in her accomplishment, the elder tells her, *Now, go and give that basket to the oldest woman in the village.* The girl's face falls. But she does as she is told. She finds the oldest woman and presents her with the basket. The oldest woman receives the basket with the grace she has gained over her long life. *You have done a beautiful thing here,* she tells the girl. *I will treasure your basket.* The girl smiles and thanks the old woman. Now the girl is a basket weaver.

ꓥ|ꓞ

pədx̌ʷayʔ (dog salmon time—November). I have driven up from Seattle to Vi's new home in Bow to collect photos. Vi says this to me as I bend to embrace her: "Today you will take a basket home with you."

"I can't do that, Vi," I say.

"You can," she says. "You will."

We take our places at her table. I see an abundance of woven cedar bark. Baskets fill three cabinets and sit atop shelves and tables. Some are as tiny as a thimble; others are large enough to carry a feast of clams and mussels gathered from nearby beaches. Surrounded by so much woven cedar, I feel sheltered, as if in a nest.

At Vi's side is a box full of sandwich bags, each one holding an item she will give away. She lifts them up to show me. Through the clear plastic of one of the bags, I see cedar bark woven into a bolo tie. In another bag is a cedar mat coaster. Names are written in big letters on tags zipped in with each item. Vi will deliver them at the next gathering. These gifts will lift the spirits of recipients for a lifetime to come.

᠊᠊᠊᠊

Vi might give a basket to a girl receiving her Indian name or being initiated into the longhouse or to a couple getting married. She might give a basket to thank a woman who has done a good work, or to encourage one to do her work.

Vi receives baskets. I have seen her give away a basket that I know was given to her. In this way, baskets journey around Indian Country.

᠊᠊᠊᠊

We are not recording one of our interviews today. I am here to borrow some photographs to accompany the article about Vi for the HistoryLink website. Vi says she can't see what's on a computer screen, no matter how large the print is. "It's okay," I tell her. "I'll print a copy for you as large as I can make it." Paper is easier, with its basketlike weave of fibers, tight enough to hold ink.

Vi has her photos out on the table. "Do you want ones of me with my men?" Her smile widens as I admire her first husband, then the next, men I have never met but who stand beside a young Vi. No color. No Photoshop. Just people wearing their best, perhaps an only suit or a dress with buttons from neck to hem and a shiny belt cinching it all in.

"You did have handsome men," I say. "Still do." We come on a picture of Vi with Don, her husband of nearly sixty years. She shrugs. It's easier to admire those no longer with us, those captured at their peak, faces full of expectation, looking out on the whole world with lives barely unfolded, capable of many imagined futures: logging, a job in Alaska, at Boeing, a turn in the service, starting a fishing business, running a café.

We look through all the photos she has out. "Where are the ones from your childhood?" I ask.

Her face closes a little. "I don't know," she says. "I can't find things since we moved up here. They were in a metal box, but I don't know where it is."

"Do you want me to help you look for it?"

"No."

So we turn back to the photos on the table: Vi wearing a cedar bark dress, Vi with a mountain goat wool shawl wrapped around her shoulders, Vi sitting on a beach holding a clam basket, its geometric cedar bark weave in her hands. I see it as a basket full of stories of how things came to be. The basket holds everything we need to know to live in this place. Vi cradles it as if it were her child.

We work our way through the photos, and then I offer to take her to lunch. "The Rhody is closed," she says. So she pours turkey soup into a saucepan and puts it on a burner. She clicks the stove to high. She stirs fast. Spoon clanks against pan. She wants it done. Now. I get up a couple of minutes later to stir the soup and lower the heat. These days, Vi can be in a hurry to do things, in a fierce race against time and infirmity. She picks up a ladle and a bowl.

"I don't think it's heated through yet, *tsi si?ab*," I tell her.

"That's okay," she says. "It doesn't need to be that hot."

"I can bring it to you." She hesitates. Then she sits back down and thanks me when I carry a white bowl filled with steaming noodles, carrots, celery, and turkey from Thanksgiving. We eat.

"I love leftover turkey," she says.

"Me too. It's the best part of Thanksgiving."

Her face is softened by wrinkles, but her eyes have a fierce strength. "I'll get us crackers." She pushes herself up from her chair. I see I need to sit and receive.

We finish lunch.

"Come visit my baskets with me," she says. She guides me to one of her tall cabinets. It is full of baskets, useful baskets, baskets to carry sweet mountain blackberries, salmonberries, or thimbleberries. Larger baskets to carry clams and mussels, maybe even oysters. Those have strong handles to lift up the sea's abundance. Platter baskets make flat ovals to hold sweet crabmeat or fresh-baked bread. A lidded basket with a cedar rope handle for carrying fish.

Vi's baskets are made of the bark or root of the western red cedar. A few baskets combine both, weaving what is below ground with what rises above. The root is the light color of winter sky or clamshell, the bark a rich, burnt red, the color of the most fertile soil, soil that has built up in layers under protection of these sentinel trees. Western red cedars line the Pacific Northwest coast and the rivers flowing down to salt water. These giants grow in the lowlands and up the slopes. Upper branches rise, towering, as if they are watching over the coastal world. Lower branches sweep down toward the earth to drop seed cones, marking a skirt around each tree. Cedar bark can be woven into a dress, a rain hat, mats for sitting on, rope, or a basket.

I wait. Vi takes a basket in her hands. "She's a good weaver. She's a relation of mine." It might be relation by blood, by marriage, or by claim. Some baskets Vi bought on her travels, perhaps to support a particular weaver she met or to remember a trip to the Olympic Peninsula or mark her stay at La Push. A whale basket helps her recall seeing a whale pass by while she and her companions hunkered down to enjoy what she called Indian Time, a luxury of winter.

Waves weave around a canoe traveling across a basket. The canoe men land a harpoon in a whale. On the other side, a whale threatens to capsize another canoe full of whalers. Woven seagulls fly overhead, not caring who wins this battle at sea. Eagle soars across another basket, wings spread, tail feathers hanging slightly down, head high, beak curved down over the woven world below. Loon, Bear, Deer, Coyote, and Salmon. All the animals are woven into these baskets, their exploits told by the weaver.

Vi tells me what she remembers about each basket. Sometimes she knows who made a basket and where. "From Quileute. From Makah." Other times, she doesn't remember, and we see if there is a strip of paper inside that will tell us. Vi's sight is nearly gone, so I read what is on the paper, small, neat script in Vi's hand from an earlier time. Each basket also has a number tag attached to it. A basket expert went through Vi's collection before she moved to Bow. I know the numbers correlate with a detailed list in a notebook. But Vi can't put her hands on the notebook just now.

After Vi holds each basket and tests her memory, she passes it to me. My hands cup the cedar basket as if it were a bird's nest. When she finishes its story, I return it to its place. We work our way down the shelves. Enough low winter sun comes through the windows to light our way.

Vi once wove a doll out of cedar bark. The doll sits on a shelf, her large head overpowering her body. "I wasn't very good." We laugh. I admire her doll. She has character and lots of brains behind her large forehead. *čəwat bibədbədaʔ* (smart dolly).

We move on to the second big cabinet and work our way down those shelves. More baskets. More stories. The light through the window thins. We keep going until we finish our journey through the second case and click the doors shut.

We make our way back to the table and sit again. Behind the table is her small cabinet of miniature baskets. The cabinet frame is dark wood with glass in front and on the sides to display treasures. Vi sits next to the cabinet and directs me from her chair. "Go choose one of those miniature baskets." She stands and guides me to the cabinet of woven wonders. She opens the doors, and then she sits.

Can I accept the gift she offers? Can I accept a basket, knowing it will travel again when my time comes? Is Vi's time coming? Am I helping her if I accept this gift?

I stand peering in at the treasures that have lived together for years. Still, I hesitate here on this winter's day in this elder's home full of treasures. I am reluctant to touch them.

In the end, she gives me no choice. "Hold each basket in your hand," she says. "One of them will speak to you." Then she speaks the command I have heard so many times when she calls on students in her classroom or at gatherings. "*haw̓ tsi si?ab* (Proceed, dear one)." There is no refusing her.

I reach out and pick up a basket barely wider than my thumb. It is tightly woven, a clamshell white with gray accent. I hold it in my palm, willing steadiness into my hand. It sits in my palm like a goldfinch egg, fragile, yet full of a whole life. I return it to its place. I see it differently now, living cedar shaped as a life is shaped.

One by one, I lift each miniature basket and cradle it, not because I want each basket or am searching for the ideal basket—the well-crafted basket, the tiniest basket, the secret basket—but because I want to hear Vi's story of each basket, want to hear her remember who wove it with her supple fingers, who gave it to Vi, or where she decided to purchase it. I long to know which basket will speak to me and am afraid of learning I might be deaf to the language of baskets. Will I hear the dry rustle of cedar bark woven into basket? Or the creak of the tightly entwined cedar root? Will I hear the cry of Crow, Raven, or Wolf woven into a basket? The smallest basket. The loveliest basket. The intended basket. You step into the world of baskets to hear all manner of stories, but the one story you overlook is the one you've always carried, the one that calls you, that allows you to hear what you were born to hear. I hold each basket close. But my basket—what is *my* basket? Am I meant to have care of a basket? Is there one basket that would finally speak? Or will they pass mutely through my fingers?

I work my way down the four shelves until I have held each and returned each to its place. With a slow breath, I admire the whole, Vi's basket collection. I listen. Then my hand moves, as if to a song. I lift up a diminutive treasure, a fine cedar root basket. Mountains weave around the basket. Each mountain links to the next, forming a line of cedar rickrack. A tiny lid fits snugly into the basket's lip. A handle no bigger than an eyelash attaches to its top. Its perfection sings.

"That's the one," Vi says. "That basket will travel home with you."

Vi Hilbert at Shilshole (photo by Paul Eubanks)

THE OTHER SIDE

Vi received messages from the other side. This often happened through the altar Vi's dad made, that familiar white wooden altar with its white cross, surrounded by a white wooden frame. Vi talked about the other side like it was the other room, just through that door, just behind that wall, or just through her altar. When I sat with her in her home, she would often point to the altar and say, "My folks came to me last night. There's work that needs to be done." And that work might be a burning to satisfy the spirit of someone on the other side or a spirit who has not fully made it to the other side, someone who is hovering. So Vi tells a ritualist that she needs to do a burning, maybe at Upper Skagit in the place where burnings are done, or at Bow or at Tulalip, or the Medicine House at Swinomish.

Sometimes a song came to Vi from the other side. But she would not sing the song, because if she did, she would have to go into the longhouse, be initiated, and be there every night of the winter spirit dance season. Her father told her this was not her work. So Vi kept that song at a distance.

But Vi felt an obligation to her parents and other relatives who had gone on to the other side. They came to her, spoke to her, guided her. She discussed all this as if she had gotten a call from living relatives. She spoke in a way that said these visitations were usual and even expected, as if crossing the divide between this world and the spirit world were not a big step.

⊓⌐

After a person dies, after the memorial service offers words and prayers and songs, after each mourner has stepped up to the open casket and spoken final words, after the casket has been closed and draped with a blanket and then placed in the hearse, after the room has emptied, but before the sun sets, a ritualist may do a burning of the beloved's closest possessions.

Helpers using dry cedar and perhaps alder will have readied the fire by the time the memorial finishes. The gathering moves to the fire. "Our loved one is still near," the ritualist says. "We need to send her special things to her so she can journey into the spirit world." This connection through fire between this world and the next can be dangerous for children or even for a vulnerable one who feels too bound to the loved one who just crossed over. Some may need to step away from this ritual fire.

The loved one's longhouse regalia may be burned, perhaps a special blanket from her bed, perhaps a dress, a shawl, a handbag, a most-often-worn flannel shirt. "She will need these things," the ritualist may say, "to ease her journey." Other possessions are given to the witnesses, possessions deemed to be safe, though later some of these may need to be burned also.

Another burning might happen a year later to send on a guitar or a carved walking stick. Sometimes even furniture is sent. Whatever the loved one has expressed a need for. Once I saw a dresser burned. And a bed. Storyteller Johnny Moses said, "Grandma Ivy won't need that. They don't sleep in the spirit world." He laughed his booming laugh. Still, the bed went to her.

If a family is bothered by a spirit who hovers too near, looking for something they need, then a burning is required. A ritualist is called in. Vi told me how her mother was asked to do this work:

"One time, there was a family being bothered by spirits who were surrounding the home with their presence. So my mother was called on to come and feel what was causing this disturbance. My mother stayed in the home and prayed and talked to the spirits. My mother said to the family, *You have something here that your loved ones on the other side want. It didn't go with them when they went to the other side. They want those things. You'll have to do a burning and let them have what they want. Then they won't be bothering you anymore here.*

"So the family listened to my mother and a spiritual fire was built. My mother came. The people brought out the things that had been the cause of the disturbance, the personal possessions of the ones who had passed over. So my mother, one by one, put these pieces on the fire that had been built for that purpose. She talked to the spirits. She said, *You folks are wanting these things. The family is giving them up so that you can have them.* I was there. I remember how beautiful the feeling was. I couldn't see or hear or feel the spirits who were being appeased. But my mother was a very vocal person, so she explained blow-by-blow what was happening. I got to feel the whole picture as it was taking place. The things that were wanted by the spirits on the other side were put on the fire and were burned. The spirits were grateful for the fact that someone had been able to hear and pay attention to their wants and needs. So from that time on, the family was no longer bothered. The spirits had received their things."

ᚾᛁᚱ

A mountain of grated cheddar grows on my cutting board. I pinch from the peak and pop it in my mouth, taste the sharp cheese. I am preparing macaroni and cheese for my father. He is on the other side. Vi invited me to offer food for him through fire at Upper Skagit. One summer Dad took us to the Tillamook cheese factory on the Oregon coast in the days when you could walk right beside the giant metal vats full of velvety milk stirred with a giant beater. He wanted us to know where cheese came from. He made macaroni and cheese for my three sisters and me whenever our mom was sick. It was what he knew how to make and it was what we loved to eat. Today I make it for him.

I arrive at the Upper Skagit Reservation and see a fire burning in an outdoor firepit. A cloth covers the ground alongside the fire, setting a table for the dead. I place the plate for my father among other plates of food at the edge of the fire. I watch the ritualist receive my dad's plate from his helper. My eyes water, my heart speeds, my hands quiver. The ritualist lifts the plate above his head and speaks my father's name—Bob Yoder. He places it on the fire as if passing it around the table. A comfort descends on me, like a shawl of memory. The fire burns the edges of the plate until it folds together. I watch the smoke rise into the pale sky.

Where is the other side, the spirit world? Is it in the sky? Where the smoke rises? Or is it through the veil? Is it visible to some? More visible as we age? They say it is the other side of something solid. Is it a comfort? A danger? Or simply the new address of our beloveds? Do we all receive messages from the other side, remembrance of the words of our ancestors, their lessons, stories, jokes, songs? Will we send messages to our people when we reach the other side?

Someone once asked Vi where the other side was. Vi shrugged her shoulders. "Beats me," she said. Yet she received guidance almost daily from that other side. Perhaps we don't need to know where the other side is, only that we may reach it via fire or prayer. Or through love.

ᖵᖶ

Vi Hilbert passed away on December 19, 2008, a night when snow blanketed western Washington. Her funeral took place over two days at the Upper Skagit Reservation. Her casket was draped with a Pendleton Legendary blanket called "Storyteller—Keep My Fires Burning."

ᖵᖶ

I received a message from Vi about six or seven months after she passed, around the time of her birthday. During the night, I heard her voice, that distinct soft voice. She told me it was now time to finish transcribing the last of our conversations. I had tried to do this earlier and it broke my heart to hear her voice on tape. She let me know that it was okay now. So I completed our work.

Vi Hilbert brings the big wave (photo by Carolyn Michael)

LUSHOOTSEED
CONTINUES

Vi Hilbert passed away December 19, 2008, but Lushootseed continues. A new generation of Lushootseed teachers and speakers are carrying it forward. Every year since Vi's passing, Lushootseed Research presents the Lushootseed Conference at Seattle University. Teachers from Tulalip, Puyallup, Muckleshoot, Sauk-Suiattle, Suquamish, and all parts of the Lushootseed world come to talk about their language programs. They show videos from their classes: Lushootseed games for young children, family conversations, or high school students rapping in Lushootseed. Suquamish teachers talk about their Lushootseed house, a place dedicated to the language. Materials and ideas are shared. These days, Lushootseed goes far beyond the classroom. One teacher uses Lushootseed in his personal training workouts. Another teaches drawing in Lushootseed. Another founds a clothing line that expresses Lushootseed. Another demonstrates how to carve a pumpkin into a jack-o'-lantern in Lushootseed. I am in awe of all of them.

Many of these teachers have been inspired by Zalmai "Zeke" Zahir. Zeke's traditional name is *Pəswəli* and I am fortunate to count him as a friend. I interviewed Zeke via Zoom on January 25, 2021, to talk about his life, his work, and about Lushootseed today.

Zeke's mother was Lou Matheson (Nakota Sioux) and his father was Asif Zahir (Afghan). His mother married his stepfather, Don Matheson (Puyallup), when Zeke was eleven. Although he was taught to appreciate his Afghan heritage, Zeke was raised in his mother's and his stepfather's traditions. It was through his stepfather that Zeke was introduced to Lushootseed. Don Matheson had heard Lushootseed growing up and had taken Vi Hilbert's class at the University of Washington, perhaps the very first one taught by Thom Hess, with Vi's assistance, using the earliest materials copied and stapled together. Over time, other members of the family also took Vi's class.

Zeke heard Don speak Lushootseed at home and asked him to teach him the language. Zeke said, "Don did spiritual ceremonies. He put his prayers into the language, some of them being quite long." This exposed Zeke to Lushootseed's connection to spirit well before he worked with Vi.

Starting when Zeke was twelve, the family lived on the Muckleshoot Reservation for four years. There he availed himself of the opportunity to learn some Lushootseed from speakers for whom it was a first language, a rare opportunity. In addition to instruction from his stepfather and from other speakers, Zeke said, "Eva Jerry taught me Southern Lushootseed in high school in 1979. I even got credit for it."

At the University of Washington, Zeke majored in civil engineering. Following in the family tradition, he took Vi's Lushootseed class. "Vi and I clicked right off the bat." Vi knew Zeke's family and knew that Zeke had studied Southern Lushootseed, so she gave him a recording of Annie Daniels telling stories, including "Fly" in Southern Lushootseed. Zeke spent the kind of time it takes to transcribe and translate. Vi was having him do what she had done and continued to do whenever she could. It was a challenging assignment and Zeke took it up. Vi and Zeke continued to work together for many years after he finished the Lushootseed class. It's clear she recognized a kindred spirit.

Zeke graduated and worked as a civil engineer, but he also kept working on the language. He realized that "if you really want to understand the culture, you have to know the language. It's the key." In 1989, he moved to Bainbridge Island. He began teaching out of his home and writing his own curriculum; he also continued to work with Vi.

For twenty years Zeke taught Lushootseed (also known in the southern dialect as *xʷəlšucid* and *txʷəlšucid*), getting people to tell stories, speak in class in a prescribed way, and maybe even sing a Lushootseed song. However, he realized something was missing: "They were not speaking it outside of class." In 2010, Zeke was accepted to the linguistics department's graduate program at the University of Oregon, where he began working on his PhD. There he did research that helped him understand the importance of motivation in language revitalization. A professor from the education department told him, "It is all about motivation. Once people are motivated to learn, your job is to keep up with them."

So, in a move toward motivation, Zeke started using a method of self-narrating daily activities to develop a home-based language nest, which is a room in your house or apartment where you only speak the language. For some it is the kitchen. You learn to say everything you do in the kitchen as you do it. *I am slicing bread, I am slicing ham, I am spreading mustard, I am washing lettuce, I am making a sandwich, I am pouring a cup of coffee.* Or your nest could be your bathroom: *I am brushing my teeth, I am washing my face, I am taking a shower, I am washing my hair, combing my hair, drying my hair,* even *I am pooping* or

I am peeing. You narrate what you do in your nest. Everything. Every day. In detail. If you wear makeup, you learn terms for eyeliner, mascara, eye shadow, foundation, blush, lip liner, lipstick, lip gloss, and all the verbs required to apply those products.

The nest becomes a room for the language. You choose a room you use regularly, where you can narrate your actions. Zeke says, "Not everyone cooks, but everyone uses the bathroom."

Zeke introduced the nest idea to seven or eight students, who all took off with it. They learned terms and discovered ways to say all the things they were doing in that room. As Zeke says, "You could feel the language living in your home." During that time, Zeke lived in an apartment where the entry door opened into the kitchen, his Lushootseed nest. So, everyone who came over to Zeke's had to manage a bit of Lushootseed if they wanted to come in. Some might have gone quickly to the living room the first time. But others might hang out in the kitchen as long as the language carried them. Perhaps further each time.

Zeke says that even if he is upset (times when language revitalizationists have noticed a decline in target language use), when he enters his kitchen, he automatically narrates each action in Lushootseed and this often shifts his mood. Lushootseed as antidepressant! Lushootseed becomes the Changer, the powerful character who comes along carrying a basket of languages and changes things from the way they were to the way they become.

After the first year of working on the nest, there was a summer break. Zeke expected some of his language nest folks might lose ground during that break. In the fall, he was delighted to find that many had jumped way ahead of where they had been in the spring. That's when Zeke realized there was something there. The nest is real. It's physical. It gives you a challenge, even a playful challenge. He says, "It's a place for the language to breathe, a place where you do not allow English." Your nest has a physical boundary. The internal motivation is turned into a daily external expectation. Zeke has written a chapter called "Language

Nesting in the Home" for the *Routledge Handbook of Language Revitalization* that explains this further. Type "Frying an egg in Lushootseed" or "Crazy for Cocoa Puffs Zalmai Zahir" into a YouTube window to watch Zeke in action in his Lushootseed nest, with the help of Cassy Fowler (George) on the Cocoa Puffs.

In addition to their language nest, Lushootseed speakers have domains, subject areas they learn to speak about. In the nest, it could be grooming or cooking. But the domains can go beyond the nest to embrace the interests of each speaker. For example, someone might choose music as a domain. Or art. Or football. Zeke tells me that one student chose Seahawks football as a domain. So, he learned to make skits about the Seahawks and narrate football games in Lushootseed. I go to YouTube and find this: "Playing Video Games in Twulshootseed!" While I am at it, I notice how much Lushootseed is on YouTube. It's astounding for a language that nearly disappeared. Zeke has the idea that a Lushootseed TV channel is in the offing.

When Zeke is training new Lushootseed teachers, he requires them to create a nest, choose domains to master, and to speak Lushootseed a certain amount of time each day. They can do it with others in person, over the phone, or now on Zoom. They start with five minutes and over time work up to an hour, then even two hours. This seems unfathomable to me. Yet Zeke has an increasing number of Lushootseed teachers who have arrived at this ability.

When Zeke moved to Eugene, Oregon, to begin working on his PhD in linguistics, Cassy Fowler (George), who had trained with Zeke to become an accomplished Lushootseed speaker, teacher, and scholar, also moved down to Eugene. They decided to become housemates so they could have a Lushootseed house. For two to three years, they spoke Lushootseed 85 percent of the time in their house. They were in regular contact with speakers of three other Indigenous languages. Though they did not all speak each other's languages, they started having support

meetings together. A Yakama elder came to one of these meetings. She spoke to all of them for a few minutes in her language,
Ichishkíin. "She told us that for the next two hours, we must
quit speaking English," Zeke says. "She was giving us direction and permission to only speak our Indigenous languages. So
we did that. You could feel your brain changing. It changes you.
Two, three, four hours of no English. By the third time we did it,
we began to understand each other. It was extremely effective.
People speaking three or four different languages, all learning
and communicating."

We talk about how it was in the old days. "Pre-contact, it was
not unusual for people to speak up to seven, eight, or more different languages," Zeke says. Intermarriage among tribes brought
automatic acquisition of a new language. And maybe you had
other relatives who spoke other languages, so you switched to
their language when you visited them. Zeke says, "When you
speak each language, you feel the world differently. Today's
education has barely caught up to pre-contact. Everyone should
experience learning at least four different languages."

Zeke talks about getting his PhD at fifty-five. The language
is his second career. And he has dealt with chronic health issues
that are sometimes debilitating. I can only imagine the effort it
took. "I did not get my PhD to make myself big," he says, "but
because I needed to do it for the language." I remind myself
that Vi suffered two aneurisms during her years of working
on Lushootseed. Both times she pushed herself to recover and
return to her work on the language.

Zeke praises the language program at Tulalip and its many
teachers. Tulalip teachers give updates on their program in person or on video each year at the Lushootseed Conference. The
program offers lots of classes for all ages at Tulalip and also at
Heritage High School and Marysville Pilchuck High School,
where Lushootseed qualifies to complete a "foreign" language
requirement. The Lushootseed section of the Tulalip website

offers resources on the language: traditional stories, how to wash your hands in Lushootseed, a calendar, the weather report, the Our Table app to guide you in Lushootseed conversation. For children, there are songs in Lushootseed ("Twinkle, Twinkle"), coloring books, games, and stories, including a Lushootseed version of *Goodnight Moon*. You can take an online lesson and download a Unicode Lushootseed font to your computer. Tulalip has opened the door to make Lushootseed accessible to all. A tremendous gift.

Zeke defended his dissertation at the same time and on the same day in 2018 that the Vi Hilbert Hall at Seattle University was dedicated. Vi's family and friends gathered along with Seattle University leaders, the architect, and the contractor to celebrate the Vi Hilbert Hall. As we were doing so, word came through that Zeke was successful. He became Dr. Zalmai "Zeke" Zahir. That day we honored Vi's work and we celebrated Zeke— his own success partly a result of that work—and we felt the radiance of a torch passing.

Zeke in turn has inspired younger tribal teachers, including those at the Puyallup Tribal Language Program, directed by Amber Hayward. These folks now teach and use Lushootseed in conjunction with their personal interests. David Sway-la Duenas, a teacher at Puyallup, is into physical fitness and is using Lushootseed in his fitness training program. Via video, you can work out with him, following his instructions and counting reps in Lushootseed. His workout is clear and his pronunciation is beyond precise. You could get fit and learn Lushootseed at the same time! I wonder how this would feel. Your backyard or a nearby park, at least for your workout, becomes your immersion into Lushootseed.

Irene McCloud (Puyallup and Nisqually) teaches Lushootseed and runs a business called Hutxh that sells clothing, some with Lushootseed messages. Hutxh offers a T-shirt that says *yəhaẃ*, which means *proceed* or *go forward*. When Vi Hilbert called on us in class, if we hesitated, she said *haẃ* (a variation of *yəhaẃ*) to bring out our response. In the story "Lifting the Sky," the word *yəhaẃ* is the command for people who speak all of these different languages to use their sticks at the same instant to lift up the sky so that it does not weigh us down. *yəhaẃ* feels like a power word, the word that will make things happen.

A hip-hop fusion musician named Calina Lawrence (Suquamish) has made a beautiful video of her song in Southern Lushootseed: *ʔəshəliʔ ti txʷəlšucid*. She fills this song with spirit and language and you can feel it lifting the sky and lifting the people.

Zeke loves that so many people are using Lushootseed in their work, their creative endeavors, and their lives. He says the language is growing faster than he ever imagined it would. We talk about where Lushootseed is and where it's showing up. "Lots of people are requesting Lushootseed in land acknowledgments." Tacoma is a hotbed. A literary publication in Tacoma called *Grit City Magazine* has a mission statement in Lushootseed in the front of every print issue. A Tacoma restaurant called Alma Mater has a Lushootseed-English menu. The City of Tacoma is partnering with the Puyallup Tribe to put up Lushootseed-English street signs. Zeke says the Puyallup Tribe has perhaps five thousand members, with about half in the region. Puyallup people who speak the language to one extent or another are interacting with non-natives, sometimes using Lushootseed. Zeke says, "It seems that Lushootseed is becoming regional."

Zeke describes having lunch and speaking Lushootseed with folks at Johnny's at Fife, near Puyallup. Other people came in who were not part of their group and greeted them and conversed in Lushootseed because they heard him and his group speaking it. Zeke tells me that Chris Briden, a Puyallup language teacher, told him that while shopping at Costco, someone came up and began speaking to him in Lushootseed. At first these unplanned language interactions are surprising. Then perhaps less surprising. I think what Zeke is saying is that there is something contagious about using the language. Language use leads to more language use, and growth is happening faster than anyone expected, including Zeke. We agree that Vi would be amazed!

Zeke is in awe of the young people he works with. He says in forty years, students like Cassy Fowler (George) will be similar to Vi Hilbert in that they will understand the very subtle linguistic interplay between speaker and environment. Zeke says he is now learning from people he once taught. "I need to live into my nineties so I can see what this group will do."

I ask Zeke if he can relate to Vi recognizing what work she had yet to do, work that only she could do. He nods. He tells me that after Vi Hilbert passed away, and then linguist Thom Hess, Zeke knew he had to step up. He is transcribing and translating some 1941 Smithsonian recordings of stories in Lushootseed. The recordings are scratchy and hard to decipher, but he goes to work. And he finds that with time and repetition, he can do it, and he may be the only one who can. He says he understands Vi better now.

There are now vibrant language programs with enthusiastic teachers. They live and work inside the language until the language lives inside of them. They take Vi's work of preserving Lushootseed and they embody it in the present in a way that will take it to the future. We can stand on the shore and call out as they pass, *lədx^wčadəx^w čələp, lədx^wčadəx^w čələp* (Where are you folks going)? Won't it be marvelous to see!

A few generations back, Lushootseed had become a trickle. There were few speakers. Vi, with the help of others, took up the work to preserve Lushootseed, and the trickle became a steady stream. Zeke, with the help of others, helped that stream grow into a river. Now the new generation is helping that river flow. Through all of these efforts, the river that is Lushootseed broadens and deepens to nourish this beautiful place, the place where the language lives.

"Zeke" Zalmai ʔəswəli Zahir (photo by Chris Duenas, courtesy Puyallup Tribal Language Program)

ACKNOWLEDGMENTS

This book came from three decades of knowing Vi Hilbert. It came from listening to her, watching how she moved in the world, how she inspired and encouraged people, how she did her work, even in the face of criticism. It is hard for me to imagine my life without Vi Hilbert. All I can say is that it would be so much less than my life with her. My gratefulness to Vi is beyond measure.

Vi Hilbert's biological family shared her with me and with others, welcomed us to family gatherings at Vi's table, in the backyard, and out at the beach property. Many of Vi's family have given their support to this book, and I would like to thank them each here: Lois Dodson (Vi's daughter) took the time to read a draft of this book and gave important help with corrections and filling in more detail. Jill La Pointe (Vi's granddaughter) and her husband, John La Pointe, read the book and made useful comments. Jill wrote the foreword and provided photos. Sasha La Pointe (Vi's great-granddaughter, marvelous writer, and carrier of Vi's traditional name—*taqʷšəblu*) also read this book and contributed to the foreword. I thank the rest of Vi's immediate family for always welcoming me: Don Hilbert and Ron Hilbert; Jay, Damas, and Lillian Samson; Bedelia Cowen; and Beau La Pointe.

Vi called many of us her Lushootseed family. We have all been there for each other and for Vi over the years. I wish to thank my Lushootseed family: Thom Hess, Dawn Bates, Pam Amoss, Andie Palmer, Alf Shepherd, Bob Hsu, Katie Jennings, Barbara Brotherton, Rebecca Chamberlain, Greg Watson, Bill Seaburg, Simon Ottenberg, Carmen Shone, Lora Pennington, Molly McGee, Sylvia Pollack, Dale Cummings, Brad Burns, Rodney Cook, Pat Twohy, Larry Blain, Marilyn Wandrey, Jack Fiander, and others. Very special thanks to Zalmai ʔəswəli Zahir, Jay Miller, Crisca Bierwert, Laurel Sercombe, Paul Eubanks, Pam Cahn, and Jill La Pointe for your essential help. Carolyn Michael and Robby Rudine, this book would not exist without each of you.

Vi called on ritualists and spiritual leaders to help her and all of us. I give thanks for them: Isadore Tom (*pətius*), Dobie Tom, Dorothy Charles, Bruce Miller, Pauline Hillaire, Kenny Moses, and Johnny Moses.

I thank extraordinary writer and teacher Priscilla Long for pushing me to write this book to the best of my ability. I also thank generous writing teachers Robert Ray, Jack Remick, and Waverly Fitzgerald.

I am blessed with support from my dear writing friends: Geri Gale, Billie Condon, Stacy Lawson, Catherine Sutthoff Slaton, Susan Knox, Pamela Hobart Carter, Arleen Williams, Sharon Goldberg, Susan Urban, Shoshana Levenberg, Corry Venema-Weiss, Kira Jane Buxton, Andrea Lewis, Elana Zaiman, Randy Hale, and Sandra Jones. My love and thanks to each of you.

Thanks to editor T. J. Hatfield, who helped pull the book together. Thanks to Amelia Schultz for proofreading at age 103. Thanks to Rita Rosenkranz, Adrienne Ross, and Bob Walls for helping me consider where the book might find a home. Thanks to Girl Friday Books for providing that home and getting the book across the threshold.

I wish to thank my parents, Bob Yoder and Elsie Yoder Forest, and my three sisters, Rebecca Gold, Gail Gilbert, and Karen Yoder. You have taught me the meaning of family.

To Robby Rudine, my love, my partner in this life, and sharer in this amazing friendship with Vi Hilbert and the world of Lushootseed, I thank you for being there always.

To all of you, and to Vi, I lift my hands in thanks.

All of the author's profits from your book purchase will be donated to Lushootseed Research to continue the work of Vi Hilbert.

(photo by Carolyn Michael)

A FEW RESOURCES

VIDEO AND AUDIO

If reading this book makes you long to move off the page to see video and hear audio of Vi Hilbert speaking, telling stories, or just being Vi, here are some places to satisfy that urge:

- "Voices of the First People: Audio and Video Recordings from the Vi Hilbert Collection" (bela. music.washington.edu/ethno/hilbert) is a wonderful sampling from Vi's recorded archive housed at the University of Washington Ethnomusicology Archives. It includes videos of her telling "Basket Ogress," "Owl and Frog," "Lady Louse," "Lifting the Sky," and "Skunk." The audio samples include early recordings of Vi working with linguist Thom Hess. You can hear her contemplate what she might do with Lushootseed one day. It also includes Vi speaking to me about starting the language work.
- *Huchoosedah: Traditions of the Heart* is a video documentary produced and directed by Katie Jennings in 1995 with KCTS and BBC Wales. It tells the story of Vi, her life's work, and how she inspired those around her. Available at vimeo.com/42640504.

- *Sharing Legends at Upper Skagit* is a video documentary of storytellers gathered by Vi Hilbert to tell their favorite stories to each other. Produced by Lushootseed Research, Vi Hilbert, and Crisca Bierwert in 1985, it is available through Internet Archive at archive.org/details/wauem2014010.
- 10wolves.com is the website of photographer and audio/video producer Paul Eubanks. You can purchase studio recordings that Paul made of Vi and others telling stories. Beautiful photos of Vi are available here also, including the one on the cover of this book.
- The Tulalip Tribes has a Lushootseed website (tulaliplushootseed.com) that provides a treasure trove of video and audio recordings of storytellers, including Vi and many others.

BOOKS OF STORIES

If this book makes you want to read more of the traditional stories, here are a few books to start you on your journey. Search a bit and you will find more.

- *Haboo: Native American Stories from Puget Sound* by Vi Hilbert (University of Washington Press, 2020)
- *Haboo: Lushootseed Literature in English* by Vi Hilbert (Lushootseed Press, 2004)
- *Mythology of Southern Puget Sound: Legends Shared by Tribal Elders* by Arthur C. Ballard (University of Washington Press, 1929) and Kenneth Greg Watson (Snoqualmie Valley Historical Museum, 1999)
- *Our Stories: Skagit Myths and Tales* by Sally Snyder (Lushootseed Press, 2002)

BOOKS BY VI HILBERT AND OTHERS

Vi loved to be at work on whatever projects felt most urgent. Many book projects came her way and she took them up with her full self. Perhaps one of her favorite projects was the "Aunt Susie" book, full title: *gʷəqʷulčəʔ Aunt Susie Sampson Peter.* Aunt Susie had a depth of knowledge that drew on the sophistication of Lushootseed and the riches of the stories. The book also includes some of the personal message recordings that Leon Metcalf made of Aunt Susie speaking to her beloved relative, messages that were then delivered when Metcalf went to visit that elder. These messages reveal an intimate use of Lushootseed, and that feeling carries across into English as well.

- *The Lushootseed Dictionary* (with Dawn Bates and Thom Hess, University of Washington Press, 1994)
- *Lushootseed Grammar Books 1 and 2* (with Thom Hess, Lushootseed Press, 1995)
- *Some Lushootseed Vocabulary from taqʷšəblu* (Lushootseed Press, 1993)
- *gʷəqʷulčəʔ Aunt Susie Sampson Peter* (with Jay Miller, Lushootseed Press, 1995)
- *siastənu "Gram" Ruth Sehome Shelton* (with Jay Miller, Lushootseed Press, 1995)
- *pətius Isadore Tom* (Lushootseed Press, 1995)
- *Ways of the Lushootseed People: Ceremonies & Traditions of North Puget Sound's First People* (with Crisca Bierwert, Lushootseed Press, 2001)
- *sdaʔdaʔ gʷəł dibəł ləšucid ʔacaciłtalbixʷ Puget Sound Geography: Original Manuscript from T. T. Waterman* (with Jay Miller and Zalmai Zahir, Lushootseed Press, 2001). This book is a treasure, especially for those who live in the Puget Sound region. You can learn the names of places and what

those names mean before you set out to visit them. It will deepen your experience of this beautiful part of the world.

VI HILBERT ARCHIVES

If you would like to research Vi Hilbert's work at the source, here is where her archives can be found:

- "Vi Hilbert Papers, 1916–2002" (accession number 5401-001) may be found at the University of Washington Libraries, Special Collections. The catalog for this archive is at archiveswest.orbiscascade.org/ark:/80444/xv54449.
- "Vi Hilbert Recordings—The Vi Hilbert Collection of Audio and Video Recordings" may be found at the University of Washington Libraries, Ethnomusicology Archives.
- There is also a Vi Hilbert Archive at Skagit Valley College.

BOOKS THAT INFORMED THIS BOOK

Many books informed this book. Here are just a few.

- *Coast Salish Spirit Dancing: The Survival of an Ancestral Religion* by Pamela Amoss (University of Washington Press, 1978)
- *Lushootseed Texts: An Introduction to Puget Salish Narrative Aesthetics*, edited by Crisca Bierwert (University of Nebraska Press, 1996)

- *S'abadeb—The Gifts: Pacific Coast Salish Art and Artists*, edited by Barbara Brotherton (Seattle Art Museum / University of Washington Press, 2008)
- *Valley of the Spirits: Upper Skagit Indians of Western Washington* by June McCormick Collins (University of Washington Press, 1974)
- *Tulalip From My Heart: An Autobiographical Account of a Reservation Community* by Harriette Shelton Dover (University of Washington Press, 2013)
- *Coast Salish Canoes* by Leslie Lincoln (The Center for Wooden Boats, 1991)
- *Shamanic Odyssey: The Lushootseed Salish Journey to the Land of the Dead* by Jay Miller (Ballena Press, 1988). Other books by Jay Miller (many available at lushootseedresearch.org) involve his work with Vi Hilbert.
- *Ron Hilbert—č'adəsq̓idəb: The Life and Work of a Coast Salish Artist* by Simon Ottenberg (Lushootseed Press, 2019)
- *Indians of Skagit County* by Chief Martin J. Sampson (Skagit County Historical Society, 1972)
- *Cedar* by Hilary Stewart (Douglas & McIntyre / University of Washington Press, 1984)
- *Salish Weaving* by Paula Gustafson (Douglas & McIntyre / University of Washington Press, 1980)
- *dxʷʔal taqʷšəblu tulʔal ti syəyaʔyaʔs: Writings about Vi Hilbert by Her Friends*, edited by Janet Yoder (Lushootseed Press, 1992)

ABOUT LUSHOOTSEED AND
LEARNING LUSHOOTSEED

If you want to know more about Lushootseed or learn Lushootseed or if you are a language geek interested in the linguistics of Lushootseed, check out the list below:

- *lushootseedresearch.org* is the website for Lushootseed Research, the organization that Vi Hilbert founded in 1983 to help preserve the language and culture. Directed by Jill La Pointe (Vi Hilbert's granddaughter), Lushootseed Research today hosts the annual Lushootseed Conference, publishes books, offers books on its website, and is making a documentary about the *Healing Heart Symphony* that Vi commissioned. The Lushootseed Research website links to the online Lushootseed dictionary, to Lushootseed fonts, to audio files for *Lushootseed Grammar Books 1 and 2* recorded by Vi, to "Voices of the First People: Audio and Video Recordings from the Vi Hilbert Collection," and much more.
- puyalluptriballanguage.org is the website for the Puyallup Tribe's language program, where you can jump right in to online lessons in Lushootseed and find lots of material.
- suquamish.nsn.us/home/departments/education1 /language-program is the website for the Suquamish Tribe's language program. It offers useful resources.
- tulaliplushootseed.com is the Lushootseed website for the Tulalip Tribes. You will find all kinds of resources, including a map of the whole Lushootseed-speaking world and a map where you can click on places to hear the pronunciation of Lushootseed names throughout the Tulalip area. The website also offers the weather report in Lushootseed, a coloring book for kids, video and

audio of traditional storytellers, language fonts, and even a conversation app called Our Table.

- Lushootseed-speaking tribes include Skagit, Swinomish, Sauk-Suiattle, Stillaguamish, Tulalip, Snohomish, Snoqualmie, Muckleshoot, Puyallup, Steilacoom, Nisqually, Squaxin Island, Suquamish, and Duwamish, and these may offer language resources on their websites.
- ais.washington.edu/fields/Lushootseed is the website for the University of Washington Lushootseed language classes.
- pugetsalish.com is the website of Zalmai "Zeke" (ʔəswəli) Zahir for Lushootseed and for the Multilingual Institute (pugetsalish.com/mi). The institute offers language classes in Lushootseed and other Indigenous languages.
- Publications by Zalmai Zahir include:
  - "Elements of Lushootseed Grammar in Discourse Perspective," PhD dissertation (University of Oregon, Eugene, 2018)
  - "Language Nesting in the Home" is a paper by Zalmai ʔəswəli Zahir included in the book *The Routledge Handbook of Language Revitalization*, edited by Leanne Hinton, Leena Huss, and Gerald Roche (Routledge / CRC Press, Taylor & Francis Books, 2018). This paper presents this innovative approach to language use.
  - puyalluptriballanguage.org/audio/puget-salish -songs-ZZ.php is the link to songs in Lushootseed put together by Zalmai Zahir. These songs may be studied and respectfully shared.
- "History of Lushootseed/dəxʷləšucid Language Instruction" is an informative paper by Laurel Sercombe published in *Journal of Northwest Anthropology*, spring 2021, vol. 55, no. 1, pp. 23–41. It covers the history of Lushootseed instruction, including Vi Hilbert's work and the work that is going on today.

- lingpapers.sites.olt.ubc.ca/icsnl-volumes is the University of British Columbia website that holds records of all of the Salish Conferences held over the years. These are linguistic papers on languages within the Salish family. Once you are on the site, type "Vi Hilbert" or "Lushootseed" into the search window and you will find lots of Lushootseed linguistic resources.
- sites.ualberta.ca/~dbeck is the website of David Beck, a linguist who worked with Thom Hess and has published linguistic articles about Lushootseed as well as republished books of stories from the Skagit Valley.
- lushootseeddictionary.appspot.com is the online version of the Lushootseed dictionary by Dawn Bates, Thom Hess, and Vi Hilbert. The online dictionary was created by linguist Deryle Lonsdale: humanities.byu.edu /person/deryle-lonsdale.
- webonary.org/lushootseed is an online dictionary primarily of Southern Lushootseed, also known as Twulshootseed (*txʷəlšucid*) or Whulshootseed (*xʷəlšucid*).
- YouTube.com: You can search "Lushootseed" on YouTube. You will find many people who are breathing life into this beautiful language.

This is not a complete list, nor is it intended to be. I hope it is a starting place. Time moves on, bringing new Lushootseed treasures. So please keep exploring.

Pəshəliʔ ti dxʷləšucid (Lushootseed lives)!

(drawing by Kenneth Greg Watson)

CITATIONS

"Where the Language Lives" first appeared in *Left Curve*, no. 29 (2005).

"Ten Things I Learned from Vi Hilbert" first appeared in *The Writer's Workshop Review*, vol. 7 (fall 2012).

"Vi Hilbert and the Gift of Lushootseed" first appeared as "Vi's Lucid Years" in *North Dakota Quarterly*, vol. 72, no. 3 (summer 2005), and *Palo Alto Review*, vol. XV, no. 2 (fall 2006).

"River Talk" first appeared in *The Raven Chronicles*, vol. 2, no. 1 (fall 1992), and *Stealing Light: A Raven Chronicles Anthology* (Raven Chronicles Press, 2018).

"*Healing Heart Symphony*" first appeared in *Sunday Ink* (Tasseomancy Press, 2010).

"Burning at Nooksack" first appeared in *The Massachusetts Review*, vol. XLVIII, no. 4 (2007).

"Wrapped in a Blanket" first appeared in *Chautauqua*, vol. 11 (2014).

"Carrying a Name" first appeared in *Ellipsis . . . Literature & Art*, vol. 48 (2012).

"Basket Song" first appeared in *The Evansville Review*, vol. XVI (2006), and *Porcupine*, vol. 10, no. 1 (2006).

IN MEMORIAM

There is no death. Only a change of worlds.
—Chief Seattle

Honor to those on the other side:
Vi Hilbert
Don Hilbert
Ron Hilbert
Thom Hess
Bob Hsu
Isadore Tom
Dobie Tom
Bruce Miller
Kenny Moses
Pauline Hillaire
Brad Burns
Amelia Schultz
Waverly Fitzgerald
Sandra Jones
Randy Hale
Shoshana Levenberg
Zen McManigal
Bob Yoder

ABOUT THE AUTHOR

© *Robby Rudine*

Seattle writer Janet Yoder took a Lushootseed class with Vi Hilbert at the University of Washington in 1978. What followed was a thirty-year friendship enduring until Vi's passing in 2008. During that time, Yoder and her husband, Robby Rudine, accompanied Vi on travels in Indian Country to attend naming ceremonies, memorials, Salish language conferences, and the observance of Treaty Day in the Tulalip Longhouse. Yoder edited two books for Vi, proofread other Lushootseed Press books, volunteered on Vi's various projects, and interviewed her extensively.

Yoder's essays and short stories have been published in literary journals, including the *Baltimore Review, Chautauqua, Jet Fuel Review, Apalachee Review, American Literary Review,* and *Passages North.* Her work has been recognized with a Pushcart Prize nomination and a Hedgebrook residency. She lives with her husband on a floating home in Seattle, Washington.

PRAISE FOR
WHERE THE LANGUAGE LIVES

"Heartfelt and honest, Yoder vividly portrays the remarkable life of this astounding woman with style and determination."
—Jay Miller, author of *Lushootseed Culture and the Shamanic Odyssey: An Anchored Radiance*

"Reading *Where the Language Lives* is like taking a long drive into Skagit Country with Vi Hilbert. I raise my hands to Janet Yoder for sharing her intimate visits with a beloved elder. Each essay is a beautifully-crafted treasure, and together they resonate as musically as an olivella shell necklace. Happiness, indeed."
—Katie Jennings, filmmaker, *Huchoosedah, Traditions of the Heart* and *The Healing Heart of Lushootseed*

"*Where the Language Lives* is a masterful presentation of the beauty and depth of Coast Salish lifeways, marvelously embodied in the life and teachings of Vi Hilbert. It is written in a flowing style, one revelation after another given just when the time is right."
—Patrick Twohy, author of *Beginnings—A Meditation on Coast Salish Lifeways*

"This book arrives like a comet, bright and beautiful, illuminating a world of wonders in the life and work of Upper Skagit elder Vi Hilbert. It should be required reading for every resident of Puget Sound Country. It is a delightful and intimate look into the life and culture of one of the most respected elders of Coast Salish territory."
—Lynda Mapes, author of *Breaking Ground: The Lower Elwha Klallam Tribe and the Unearthing of Tse-whit-zen Village*

"*Where the Language Lives* is a profound and stunning book that captures the spirit of the treasured Upper Skagit elder Vi Hilbert with love and richness of detail. [. . .] Written with grace and insight [. . .] it chronicles the Indigenous culture that Vi Hilbert helped to preserve, which she shared over three decades with author Janet Yoder, among many others. If you live anywhere in the Pacific Northwest, you must read this book."
—Priscilla Long, author of *Fire and Stone: Where Do We Come From? What Are We? Where Are We Going?*

"Janet Yoder's writing captures the spirit of this honorable and mischievous elder. In Lushootseed culture, words are spoken and stories are told without explanation. Words mean what the listener hears. You learned to be careful what you said in the presence of *taqʷšəblu* [Vi Hilbert]—you may have just made her a promise. A tribute to the life of a revered elder on a mission to save her language—all that is missing are more of *taqʷšəblu*'s 'R-rated' stories."

—*dxʷtuk kʷi at kən* (Jack Fiander), *taqʷšəblu*'s longtime attorney and former student

"In *Where the Language Lives*, Janet Yoder weaves a strong, beautiful basket filled with stories of Upper Skagit elder Vi (*taqʷšəblu*) Hilbert's remarkable life and work. [. . .] These essays (and photos) reveal Vi's warmth, determination, and generosity and show her single-minded focus on resurrecting Lushootseed, the language of many of the Pacific Coast First People. [. . .] If you never had the good fortune to meet Vi, to hear her tell the story of Lady Louse, or to feel the warmth of her welcome, this generous book will introduce you to her and her work. For those of us who did know her, it is a shining testament to an extraordinary woman."

—Sylvia Byrne Pollack, author of *Risking It*

"Vi Hilbert was a wisdom keeper and cultural treasure. If she'd had a mantra, it would have been 'Stand up and speak.' Janet Yoder stood side by side with Vi for decades, as her sometimes driver and frequent chronicler. Yoder vividly brings Vi's generous spirt alive and magnifies her timeless work to keep Indigenous language and culture strong and enduring."

—Ward Serrill, filmmaker and author of *To Crack the World Open: Solitude, Alaska, and a Dog Named Woody*

"*Where the Language Lives* is a warm woven blanket of a book. With rich and reverent storytelling, Janet Yoder gifts us with stories of Upper Skagit tribal elder Vi Hilbert, continuing Vi's tradition of deep generosity while sharing lessons of language and life, community and connection, family and faith. This book lifted my spirits, held my heart, and spoke to me in a universal language—love."

—Kira Jane Buxton, author of *Hollow Kingdom* and *Feral Creatures*